Planning for Tomorrow

Your Passport to a Confident Future

I wish for you a
long + well-planned
life.

Linda

Linda S. Thompson

ISBN: 0-9764903-0-7
First Printing   January 2005

This publication is designed to provide accurate and authoritative information with regard to the subject matter covered. It is sold with the understanding that the author is not engaged in rendering legal, financial, or other professional advice. If legal advice or other expert assistance is required, the services of a competent professional should be sought.

- From a *Declaration of Principles* jointly adopted by a
Committee of the American Bar Association
and a Committee of Publishers and Associations

Printed in the U.S.A. by
Lightning Source Inc. (US)
1246 Heil Quaker Blvd.
Al Vergne, TN USA 37086
1-615-213-5815

This book is dedicated to my mother, Frances Frazier. If she were not sharing her journey with me, this book, *Planning for Tomorrow*, and the *life planning* concept could not exist.

- Linda S. Thompson

Acknowledgments

My entrée into the world of *life planning* was happenstance at best. After more than 30 years in marketing, and experiencing corporate downsizing more times than I can count, it became very clear that if I were going to attain the level of independence I was striving for, I would have to have my own business. Add to that my mother and I reaching the decision to share a home, and it now seems almost pre-ordained that *Planning for Tomorrow* would come into existence.

Many people have touched my life in various ways from the incidental to the very profound. While it would be impossible to name them all, those who have provided inspiration, support and encouragement for my endeavors have been and remain very important in my life. My best friend from middle school and forever, Diana O., has always been there for me and without her love and friendship, I would not be the woman I am today. I'd like to thank my one-time co-worker and continued dear friend, Sandi M., who is my "best buddy," my sounding board, and my sanity check, Sue S. who has supported me with excellent advice, constant support and true friendship, and Connie W., without whom my dream would never have become a reality. And to all of the others who have touched my life in so many different ways, those who have offered friendship and most of all that very important kick in the backside whenever they saw me slipping from my goals. You know who you are, and I thank you.

Table of Contents

Table of Contents (Cont'd.)

Table of Contents (Cont'd.)

Introduction

Right after September 11, 2001, I began one of my lectures with, "On September 11, how many people kissed their family good-bye and set off to work secure in the knowledge that they would be having dinner with their family that night? How many didn't? How many families lost their homes due to the loss of income? How many children's college educations have been jeopardized because a father or mother believed, 'it won't happen to me?'" It's those little, and sometimes not so little, occurrences that wreak havoc with how we think our lives will play out.

When you think of creating your *life plan*, what comes to your mind first?

- *Dull and boring?*
- *Too difficult to tackle?*
- *Uncomfortable?*
- *I don't know where to start?*

You purchased this book for a reason. Perhaps it was just something to add to the collection of unread books, on your list of "things I should read," placed on your bookshelf or nightstand. It is my goal to show you that *life planning* can be:

- *Rewarding and informative,*
- *Not terribly time-consuming if taken one step at a time,*
- *A way to open communication and offer the opportunity to enter into quality conversations with family members,*
- *A method of providing a sense of security and peace of mind upon completion.*

We "boomers" are notorious for the Scarlett O'Hara philosophy of, "I'll think about it tomorrow." When you picked up this book, you took the first step toward developing your plan. You've decided that your tomorrow has arrived and it's time to get started. You have made a commitment to yourself and to your family and friends to get your house in order. Congratulations!

Have you ever asked yourself at what age you think you will die? Not a comfortable question, is it? But ask it of yourself now. What was your immediate, off the top of your head response? Now look at that age in the context of your life as it is now. Are you prepared for it to happen should it happen when you predict?

What fears and uncomfortable feelings come to mind when you think about your eventual demise? It's a well known fact of life that we're all going to die, whether or not we plan for it. Wouldn't you feel much more secure in your own mind if you knew your family would be taken care of?

As you work your way through this book, you will find that *life planning* is not all financial and legal. It's not all boring, and it certainly isn't all doom and gloom. Did you know that those of us who follow the current senior generation have the potential of living longer after retiring from our primary career than we spent in our primary career? What does the next chapter of your life hold? Some things to think about:

- Am I cultivating relationships with people younger than me? This is important – what will the quality of your life be if you outlive the people in your circle of peers?

- What are you going to do? And I don't mean sleep late then go play golf. The days ahead will be long, boring and at times even depressing, if we don't have a purpose; a reason to get out of bed in the morning. Perhaps you will choose volunteer or community service work; perhaps a less demanding place to work allowing you a measure of autonomy not currently available in your current position? How about starting your own business?

- Do you see travel in your future? If so, do you have the funds to support those adventures?

My purpose for writing this book is to help each and every one of its' readers understand that life can be rewarding, fulfilled and a "fun time" if we allow ourselves the luxury of thinking about it, visioning it, and if looked upon with a sense of anticipation, not dread.

While this book and my company focus primarily on the baby Boomer generation (those born between 1946 and 1964), in reality the subject matter is pertinent to every age. The details may change slightly and the circumstances may vary as everyone travels their individual journey down a path that has many forks in the road, but inevitably we all end up in the same place.

From the time we are children, we have begun to collect that inevitable stack of paper that identifies us to the outside world. Deep inside, we know exactly who we are. The rest of the universe has no idea unless we have a name, a birth certificate, a social security number, and on and on and on.

After birth, as we grow, graduate from school, leave our parents' home, get married, and have children, our stack of paper grows. We now have diplomas, marriage licenses, and perhaps divorce decrees, medical records, insurance policies, deeds and titles to property we own, and even more. All this paperwork can become overwhelming and unless you are one of the extremely organized people I've met over the years, you will spend hours trying to find and organize your "paper identity." In a later chapter, we will talk about what paper is necessary and why, and what to do with it after we have it.

But *life planning* isn't just about paper. Throughout this book, we're going to address the various stages of adult life and discuss methods of surviving each. How do we plan our lives so they become what we want and not what everyone around us thinks we should have or need? What personal observations have you made over the years that contribute to who you are? You will find areas set aside for your questions, observations and reminders. Remember that this book is meant to be a living document, and living means change. With each stage of your life, the contents of this book will take on a different meaning and your paper identity will increase, decrease or be revised in some way.

As you work your way through your personal *life planning* experience, you may come across some disturbing issues you need to address. I've intentionally designed it to make you think. That's part of the plan – life isn't always easy, and planning for the not-so-easy parts is something we tend to avoid. My goal is to pass along to you common sense and sound reasons why avoidance is not the ideal method of handling a problem or preparing for your future.

Also included are personal stories because I believe if the subject is personalized, it becomes less overwhelming and perhaps just a bit easier to face. It's the trial and error, the adventures and the wrong turns that make us human and my mother and I have experienced a lot of them. I've drawn on the experiences of my friends and colleagues for their stories as well. The uplifting and the heartbreaking – they are part of the very fabric of our lives. Don't be hesitant to write down some of your own stories. Our perspective changes over the years and though a chapter in your story might be sad at this point in time, it may bring laughter in a few years. So much of who we are from generations past has been lost because we didn't take the time to listen, to record the story, to pay attention to what was being offered. Don't let that happen to you.

Up to this point, you're probably wondering if this entire exercise is going to be serious and at times depressing. No, that is not the case. I've added humor throughout, because humor and laughter are so important to our well being. Our journey must be enjoyed.

With that, I will offer the following ways of dealing with the burdens of life.

- Accept that some days you're the pigeon, and some days you're the statue.

- Always keep your words soft and sweet, just in case you have to eat them.

- Always read stuff that will make you look good if you die in the middle of it.

- Drive carefully. It's not only cars that can be recalled by their maker.

- If you can't be kind, at least have the decency to be vague.

- If you lend someone $20 and never see that person again, it was probably worth it.

- Never put both feet in your mouth at the same time, because then you won't have a leg to stand on.

- Nobody cares if you can't dance well. Just get up and dance.

- Since it's the early worm that gets eaten by the bird, sleep late.

- The second mouse gets the cheese.

- When everything's coming your way, you're in the wrong lane.

We worked furiously to realize our goals. Because we did not have fear, we could do something drastic.
> - Masaru Ibuka, Founder, Sony Corp. 1991

To make your *life planning* experience as successful as possible, I'm asking you to cast aside any fear you may have, and as Mr. Ibuka said, "do something drastic."

Chapter 1

The Aging of America

We're the rock-n-roll – not the rockin' chair – generation!!!!
- Linda Meissner

There are 76 million baby boomers nearing retirement age and this country is woefully unprepared for the challenges we bring. If you think that's frightening, try this on for size. By the year 2030, there will be 400 MILLION elderly people in China, and only 1 in 4 have any type of retirement plan at all. What's the difference between China and us? The U.S. became rich before it got old – China will become old long before it gets rich. This is a world crisis of major proportions and we don't seem to be taking it seriously.

As hard as it is for all of us to admit, aging isn't an option. However, the way we go about it and whether or not we plan for it is. Medication prices are skyrocketing, and with those medications comes extended life, but at what cost to the quality of life and most especially to our dignity. We baby boomers didn't take particularly good care of ourselves physically and the unknown health consequences are still on the horizon. We've spent at the rate we've earned, and the odds of outliving our money are great. So where will our helping hand come from?

Who will provide the care I may need as I age? And of those I name below, are they aware of my wishes and will they be around when I need them? _____
_____
_____
_____
_____

We pay our athletes astronomical amounts of money to play games, but we don't pay our health care providers and our caregivers a living wage. There are resources and services available in metropolitan areas, but those in rural communities must rely on families who frequently live great distances from their elders. Today, the majority of our caregivers are over the age of 45. Who will fill their shoes in the coming years?

NOTE: In 1900, life expectancy at birth was 47.9 for males and 50.7 for females. In 2000, life expectancy at birth was projected to be 74.1 for males and 79.5 for females.
Source: The MetLife Mature Market Institute, Demographic Profile of American baby boomers, 2003

Assisted living care today costs an average of $36,000 per year and is projected to increase ten fold in the next 20 years. Will you have $360,000 to pay for one year of care? I do strongly advise everyone I consult with to get long-term care insurance if they can qualify. A lot of us wait until it's too late, health problems have been diagnosed and long-term care insurance is no longer an option. What about a will, a living will, and/or advanced directives? Do you have any of these? They are all part of a *life plan*.

Do I have any or some of these documents?		
Long-term Care Insurance	❑ Yes	❑ No
Funeral Plan	❑ Yes	❑ No
Life Insurance	❑ Yes	❑ No
Powers of Attorney	❑ Yes	❑ No
Advanced Health Care Directives	❑ Yes	❑ No
Will and/or a Trust	❑ Yes	❑ No

Contrary to popular belief, the attitude of, "if I don't talk about it, it won't happen," is wrong. It will! For those of us who have chosen the single route with no children, we must consider, "who will be me for me?" For those of us with families, we worry about becoming a burden on them.

Will Social Security and Medicare exist 10 to 20 years from now as it does today? There are fewer and fewer people funding the system and more and more people are becoming dependent on that same system. And can we realistically count on a program that is controlled by those who are not dependent upon it? We must look at every aspect of the lives we treasure now and have the courage to realistically evaluate the quality of those lives during the latter stages of our journey.

ACTION CANCELS FEAR EVERY TIME!

I've been in the elder care industry for nearly five years and have earned the equivalent of a Ph.D. in understanding the difficulties associated with aging. Did you ever watch an older person struggle to get in and out of a car? I don't know about you, but I struggle to get into an SUV now. How about their inability to comprehend all of the latest technology? Hard as I may, teaching my 89 year old mother how to use a computer was a major challenge; and one that was unsuccessful. What will challenge us when we reach that age?

What are some of the recent observations I've made when seeing an elderly person (our parents, our in-laws, or someone we don't even know) in a restaurant, a supermarket, getting in and out of a car? Did I give it a second thought – that one day that could be me?_____

I've gained firsthand experience living with Mom and watching her go from a very independent woman who didn't quit a full-time job until age 76, to a lady who has balance problems and can't walk without help, who no longer has the confidence to balance her own checkbook and still doesn't understand how her ATM card can also be used like a credit card. She no longer drives and that loss of independence is heartbreaking. She's been frustrated, discouraged, and depressed at no longer being able to do the things she used to do with ease. I can't tell you how many times she has said, "I never thought I'd get to the place where I couldn't take care of myself." Can I see myself walking in her shoes? You bet I can! Does it frighten me? You bet it does!

Judith Regan said, *"The key to successful aging is to pay as little attention to it as possible."* That is not the best advice for any of us. Granted, we don't want to dwell on all the negative aspects of aging, and we really would like to look forward to our next chapter with anticipation. However, what our next chapter holds in store for us depends a great deal on what we do about it now.

Recently I took Mom on a trip to the Midwest for the funeral of her sister. We had to fly half way, then drive another six hours to reach our destination. Our departure airport was surprisingly "senior friendly" although our security people still haven't grasped the difference between the elderly and the handicapped. What happens to the person who can navigate with a walker, but cannot walk unaided through the security checkpoint? It was obvious that this situation had not been considered in the design of their system. Our destination airport, on the other hand, hadn't a clue. Designed to move a lot of people, they thought only about moving people who could move themselves. Electric carts can get you with ease from the arrival gate to the baggage claim, but there are too few to meet the need. A traffic jam of carts waiting for the one elevator was constant. Shuttle vans from the airport to the car rental facilities are a hazard for anyone who can't navigate the high steps in and out of those vans. The assumption seems to be that unless you are in a wheelchair, you can get from point A to point B with no assistance.

And if you use a walker to assist you, you're an accident waiting to happen. Has it ever occurred to restaurants and motels that door jambs are a hazard? Wouldn't it be just as easy to design mini-ramps in lieu of the current barricades?

Is anyone in your family currently mobility-challenged? If so, can you see yourself in their shoes as you grow older? What are you willing to do now to change what needs changing? _____

_____

_____

_____

After the challenges over those five days travel, Mom has decided that traveling is no longer worth the effort. How many other mobility-challenged people reach that conclusion? What does that sense of defeat do to their quality of life? What will it do to ours when it's our turn?

And so I ask you, what can we do to ensure our future is one of freedom rather than confinement; one of comfort rather than one of hazard? We need to speak out about what we see, what we hear and what we personally experience. I've written letters to airports, hotels and restaurants as a result of my trip with Mom. If we all take the attitude that one person can't instigate change, then where will change come from? One voice at a time will start to promote an awareness of where our country, and the world, is heading and what services need to be considered. However, we must be extremely cautious with the programs we design today, as they are the programs we will be using tomorrow.

Mom is becoming more mobility challenged every day. She has balance and stability problems and is unable to walk down the hall without her walker or holding on to both sides of the wall. Although we have installed a hand-held shower head and put a seat into the tub, she is no longer able to safely step into the bathtub to take a shower, even seated. Fortunately, I recently met a gentlemen who has started his own business retrofitting homes to meet the needs of the mobility-challenged. A simple solution of a swivel seat that attaches to the tub has solved the problem for now. When we built our home, we weren't thinking of the possible eventuality of her being in a wheelchair. Our doors are not wide enough to accommodate one. There were no handhold bars in the bathrooms for her to hang on to, and the three inch drop from the family room out onto the patio has become a hazard for her. All of these things are having to be addressed as she ages and, once again, I am fortunate enough to know the people who can help us with these problems.

Unfortunately, not everyone will have ready access to solutions for such challenges of daily living. Isn't it time to take a stand with our builders, contractors, architects, and others in the industry? Isn't it time to not just ask, but demand, those issues be addressed? Like it or not, all of us will probably end up needing one, if not more, of these aids or our independence will be severely limited. And those are just issues for the aging; what about those of you who have mobility-challenged spouses or children at home? Do the same issues not affect you as well? We have been all too willing to accept what has been given us without ever questioning the possible need for improvements. We need to change our attitude of acceptance and not be afraid of asking that our current and future needs be addressed.

Will each of you become just a bit more aware of your surroundings? Will you speak out when you see a need that is not being met, and most of all, talk to your families about what you want your future to hold? We need to accept responsibility for our own well-being and realize that our growing numbers will add an ever-increasing burden to an already overwhelmed and woefully inadequate system.

We boomers are, after all, 76 million strong. And unless we lived in a cave in the 70's, we know how to bring about change. Are we

going to do something about this looming crisis? It's in your hands
– it is, after all, your future.

> What am I willing to do to promote change for myself and my peers?
> Am I willing to exchange my independence for silence or will I speak out
> when I see a need that is not being met?_____
>
> _____
>
> _____
>
> _____

And because life should not be all serious, how about this for
planning?

The Holiday Inn Retirement Plan

Finally, a RETIREMENT PLAN that makes sense:

Recently I was checking my 401(k) account and thinking about retirement,
as everyone does when they hit 50 (or mid-40's) or even 60!

I saw an article about Nursing and Retirement Homes and the expenses.
Then it hit me; here is my plan.

No nursing home for me! I'm checking into the Holiday Inn. With the average
cost for a assisted living reaching $188.00 per day, there is a better way
when we get old and feeble. I have already checked on reservations at the
Holiday Inn for a combined long-term stay discount and senior discount,
its $49.23 per night.

That leaves $138.77 a day for: Breakfast, lunch, and dinner in any restaurant
I want, or room service, laundry, gratuities, and special TV movies. Plus,
they provide a swimming pool, a workout room, a lounge, washer, dryer,
etc. Most have free toothpaste and razors, and all have free shampoo and
soap.

They treat you like a customer, not a patient. Five dollars worth of tips a day will have the entire staff scrambling to help you. There is a city bus stop out front, and seniors ride free. The handicap bus will also pick you up if you fake a decent limp. Ride the church bus free on Sundays.

For a change of scenery, take the airport shuttle bus and eat at one of the nice restaurants there. While you're at the airport, fly somewhere.

Otherwise, the cash keeps building up. It takes months to get into a decent assisted living facility. Holiday Inn will take your reservation today. And you are not stuck in one place forever, you can move from Inn to Inn, or even from city to city.

Want to see Hawaii? They have a Holiday Inn there, too. And Mexico, and France, and Japan.

TV broken? Light bulbs need changing? Need a mattress replaced? No problem. They fix everything and apologize for the inconvenience.

The Inn has a night security person and daily room service. The maid checks if you are OK. If not, they will call the undertaker or an ambulance. If you fall and break a hip, Medicare will pay for the hip, and Holiday Inn will upgrade you to a suite for the rest of your life.

And no worries about visits from family. They will always be glad to visit you, and probably check in for a few day's mini-vacation. The grandkids can use the pool. What more can you ask for? So, when I reach the golden age I'll face it with a grin.

Just forward all my e-mails to the Holiday Inn!

Upon telling this story at lunch with friends, we came up with even more benefits the Holiday Inn provides to retirees:

Most standard rooms have coffee makers, reclining chairs, and satellite TV – all you need to enjoy a cozy afternoon. After a movie and a good nap, you can check on your children (free local phone calls), then take a stroll to the lounge or restaurant where you meet new and exotic people every day.

Many Holiday Inns even feature live entertainment on the weekends. Often they have special offers, too, like the Kids Eat Free Program. You can invite your grandkids over after school to have a free dinner with you. Just tell them not to bring more than three friends.

Pick a Holiday Inn where they allow pets, and your best friend can keep you company as well. If you want to travel, but are a bit skittish about unfamiliar surroundings, in a Holiday Inn you'll always feel at home because wherever you go, the rooms all look the same.

And if you're getting a little absent-minded in your old days, you never have to worry about not finding your room—your electronic key fits only one door and the helpful bellman or desk clerk is on duty 24/7.

Being natural skeptics, we called a Holiday Inn to check this story out. I'm happy to report that they were positively giddy at the idea of us checking in for a year or more. They even offered to negotiate the rate (we could have easily knocked them down to $40 a night!).

See you at the Inn!

Source: Author unknown; this was sent to me in an e-mail message in 2003.

Chapter 2

If it's a Journey, Where's the Road Map?

That which we persist in doing becomes easier for us to do – not that the nature of the thing has changed, but that our power to do is increased.

- Ralph Waldo Emerson

Let's first set the stage for this chapter. Below are four examples of life that may or may not ring true for you right now. However, at some point in your life, one, if not more, will either directly or indirectly touch your life.

Case 1:

You have a young family; two children, age 2 and 7. You and your spouse have recently purchased a new home and are going out tonight to celebrate, leaving the kids with a baby-sitter. On the way home, a car accident kills you both. What happens now? Have you discussed who will raise your kids if you aren't there to do it? Is that decision in writing? Do you have life insurance that will take care of your children's financial future including higher education? Or if only one of you survived, could the other keep the home, raise the kids and maintain any kind of quality of life financially? What if you were on life support – does your spouse know what your beliefs are – do you want to be kept on life support, or do you wish to go with dignity? If you live, but your quality of life is severely impaired, do you have long-term disability and/or long-term care insurance to cover at least a part of the costs? And last but most certainly not least, does the baby-sitter know who to call if you don't come home?

Case 2:

You are an only child, your father is deceased, and your mom is living on her own in a nearby town. You receive a call from Mom's neighbor that she has fallen and is being taken by ambulance to the hospital. By the time you get there, Mom has had a stroke and slipped into a coma. Do you have medical power attorney to make decisions on her behalf? Do you have financial power of attorney to pay her bills while she's unable to? Do you even know what bank she uses, whether or not she has long-term care insurance, or has made out a will? If the worst should happen, have you discussed what her wishes are for the end of her life and her funeral?

Case 3:

Your house just burned to the ground. Do you have your documents in a fire proof safe, a safety deposit box, or at the very least, do you know the names and contact numbers of your insurance agent(s), your credit card companies, etc. How about purchase receipts and warranties on large purchases? Most of us just toss this stuff as soon as we take the new big screen TV out of the crate. But what happens if you need to provide proof of purchase? Perhaps your grandmother's sterling silver tea service was in that fire – do you have an appraisal, a photo, anything to offer as proof of ownership and value to your insurance company?

Case 4:

You and your spouse are approaching retirement and neither is in extremely good health. Thirty years ago you had a child that has been severely handicapped all his life and has lived his entire life in a facility designed to care for his disabilities. Although you believe you have put aside sufficient funds to care for this child through his projected lifespan, you and your spouse are worried about his care once the two of you are gone. What preparations have you made to cover this inevitability? Who have you entrusted to ensure payments for your child's care are made on time, and will they continue to do so once you are no longer there to monitor their performance?

These examples happen every day of the week somewhere in the world. *Life planning* is all about preparation for life's crises, the unexpected and the inevitable. Consider how many young parents went to work the morning of September 11, 2001 thinking they would be having dinner with their families that night. What are the long-term consequences of poor or no planning?

> Is my life reasonably organized? ❑ Yes   ❑ No
> What are my next steps to ensure my family knows what I want and where the documentation is? _____
> _____
> _____

Let's talk a bit about wills and trusts and the need for one if not both. This topic is for all ages and that includes the young man just going off to college and who has a very valuable coin collection, the young couple who have recently had a baby, the father just diagnosed with Alzheimer's, the empty nester, the elderly and everyone in be-tween. No one is exempt from the need to create a plan.

Why is this so important? Because of what happens when you don't plan. In Case 1, the courts could, and probably would, take cus-tody of your children, then a judge would determine what's best for them. Is that what you want? How could a judge possibly deter-mine what would be best for your family — (s)he is, after all, a total stranger to you. Wouldn't it be better to plan for disaster and have nothing happen than to not plan and to lose it all?

In Case 2, will you find out after Mom has been put on a respirator that she wanted no heroic measures taken; that she wanted to pass peacefully with no intervention with her dignity intact? If she survives the stroke and needs care provided at a nursing home, are there sufficient funds to finance her care? What if the same thing happened to you?

Things to consider for my loved ones, and my own well-being.

Life Insurance – If I have a policy, is the death benefit sufficient in today's dollars? _____

_____

Supplemental Disability Insurance – Does this make sense for my family? _____

Long-Term Care Insurance – What happens to me or my loved ones if there are inadequate funds to pay for necessary care?

_____

_____

_____

All of this sounds daunting, but believe me, a person who has prepared for those possibilities is much better equipped to handle a crisis situation than one who has not.

A Will

A will is the legal document you use to outline how you want your property and assets divided among your family members and other heirs. In your will, you can also name guardians for your children. Your will should identify who you want to serve as the executor of your estate.

NOTE: When you name guardians for your children and the executor of your estate, make absolutely sure that those named are aware of your wishes and are willing to accept the assignment.

A Basic Living Trust

With a basic living trust, you transfer the ownership of all your assets and property to a trust. The assets in a living trust don't have to go through the costly, time-consuming – and public – process of probating your estate in state court. The trust assets can pass directly to the beneficiaries you designate. You can appoint yourself as both trustee and primary beneficiary so that you can maintain complete control over the trust before your death.

NOTE: There are many different types of trusts; some more applicable to your particular situation than others. We urge you to work with an estate planning attorney to help you determine what is best for you and your family.

After you have completed the basics of your plan, you need to make your plan effective. Remember that this is a living document and that from time to time your situation may change with marriage, divorce, children, death and so on. It is a good idea to review your plan on an annual basis and update the information as needed.

The following are steps to take to make your plan as effective as possible.

1. Keep your intentions clear

   a. Write a letter of instruction to let your family members know what initial steps they should take after you are gone.

   b. Keep your will current.

   c. Ensure the appropriate people know where your documents are located.

2. Avoid common mistakes

   a. Leaving everything to your spouse may seem like the simplest thing to do, but it can increase the taxes that your estate will incur when it eventually passes to your children or other heirs.

   b. Holding assets jointly with children – putting anyone other than your spouse as joint owner of an account can create unexpected problems. For example, you want to make sure your daughter gets your house after your death, so you list her on the property title, the deed. A few years later, she is in a car accident and is sued for damages. Because on paper she owns half of your home, should she lose the case, you could find yourself without a roof over your head.

3. If you are unmarried

   a. Remember that property shared by unmarried couples is generally governed by contract, not family, law. In English, if you die, your partner – unlike a spouse – won't have any legal rights to assets or property on which they were not a registered legal owner.

   b. Have a will and consider using trusts to protect your partner

4. Take several steps on your own

   a. Designate beneficiaries for your IRAs, pension, and life insurance and keep your designations up to date

   b. Use Transfer on Death (TOD) registrations for mutual funds, stocks or bonds as you cannot name beneficiaries on these types of investments.

5. Prepare for incapacity

   As part of your plan, you will also want to take steps to protect your family if you become seriously ill or disabled. The following tools have been created to assist you under these circumstances:

a. Long-term care insurance

b. A durable power of attorney

c. A health care proxy

d. A living will

The significant problems we face cannot be solved by the same thinking that created them."

- Albert Einstein

NOTE: Refer to Appendix A for further information on financial issues and to Appendix B for estate planning.

Now that the boring stuff is taken care of, let's talk a bit about what you are going to do with your "Second Middle Age." Lydia Bronte, a New York gerontologist and author of *The Longevity Factor: The New Reality of Long Careers and How it can Lead to Richer Lives,* 1993, suggests that a longer life span creates a "second middle age." It's not that we're older longer; in essence, we're middle-aged longer, thanks in part to the slowing of the aging process. We can fully engage in life and continue our pursuits. We have the added benefit of life experience and the wisdom that accompanies that. She indicated that the majority of those she interviewed for the book started their greatest period of creativity and productivity at age 50 or later.

Baby boomers are the first generation in American history whose average member will live into their 80s, experts say. An avalanche of Boomer octogenarians is approaching. Now there are 9 million Americans 80 or older; in 2025, there will be 15 million; by 2050, 31 million, the Census Bureau estimates.

But will those elders feel truly old? One-third of Americans in their 70s said they considered themselves "middle-aged," as did 22% of those 80 or older, in a Harris Interactive survey in 2004 for the National Council on Aging.

What Boomer doesn't recall that wistful question wailed by The Beatles?

Will you still need me
Will you still feed me
When I'm 64?

When we first heard this song, 64 seemed ancient. Today we put that number in an entirely different perspective. Isn't it amazing what a few years will do?

I married you for better or for worse, not for lunch!

You may laugh when you read this, but it's definitely something to think about. Humorous but true. Put yourself in the following place:

You've worked all your life to support your wife and family. You've purchased several homes, each one a bit bigger and a bit better. You're driving nice cars, both kids are in college and you and your wife are now living in an "empty nest." You have more than adequate savings to feel secure and enough to fund those unexpected emergencies. You're pretty pleased with yourself—you've made it! By all accounts, you're considered successful.

For the first time in 20 years, your wife is free to have lunch with her friends, shop whenever she chooses and take her time doing so. She may spend a few hours at a day spa, or she may enjoy reading the latest book by the pool. Perhaps she's thinking about pursuing a career; after all, the kids are gone and she's still healthy and active.

You come home one day and announce that you've decided to retire. You've always dreamed of traveling the country in a big RV and are so excited you can barely contain your enthusiasm. You're thinking of selling the house, downsizing and living 12 months out of the year in this RV. You look across the table at your wife and she's turned white; she looks like she could be sick any minute and you wonder what's wrong.

The details may be different, but this scene has been played many times over in households across the country. While you were busy with your career, and your wife was busy caring for the family, the two of you forgot about each other. What do you have in common? Now that the kids are gone, what do you talk about across the dinner table? Do you share common friends with common interests, or has your social life been directly related to your career?

Perhaps your idea of the perfect retirement is to sleep late, have brunch while reading the paper, watch a bit of TV, play a round of golf, have dinner, watch a bit more TV and off to bed. While this may be your dream, it most likely is your wife's nightmare. She envisions you under foot all day, expecting her to cook meals for you. She's thinking she just got rid of the kids, has just started enjoying life, and now is facing another "kid" underfoot. This could be a divorce waiting to happen if open communication doesn't exist.

Now you see why I say it's not all legal and financial, i.e., boring stuff. But it is all about *life planning*. Failure to plan leads to disappointment. Disappointment leads to anger, and anger in turn leads to depression. One of the biggest health problems in our senior population today is depression.

It's never too late to renew that friendship, that feeling of companionship, and especially that feeling of excitement the two of you had when you first started out. Somehow, you let life get in the way, but it can be corrected. Start by talking about how each of you envision the next chapter in your lives. It may be that you both want to travel, that you both have a shared interest in volunteerism or some sort of community service. More likely, though, each of you have a mental vision of your next chapter in life and it may not be the same vision your partner has.

Compromise and negotiation will be necessary. Agree to disagree on some things and recognize the need for agreement on others. Perhaps you agree to take separate vacations every year—you to the latest golf course and your wife to the beach with her friends. Contrary to popular belief, twenty-four hour togetherness is not utopia for everyone.

We baby boomers will be the first generation in history that could and very well may live as long after our primary career as we did during that career. That's a long time to live with no plan. I don't know of anyone who could drift along, letting life take its course for 30+ years, do you? Wouldn't it be better to begin discussions now about how you want to spend those years? Remember the song, *What are You Doing the Rest of Your Life?* The planning should start today.

Throughout my research for this book, I've come across a few points that are continuously mentioned when speaking of successful aging. They are:

- Maintain high mental and physical function. Exercise of the brain is as important as exercise of the body.

- Be actively engaged with life. Join a club, attend church, get involved with community groups, take part in service organization activities.

- Unleash your creativity; write a book, get out that camera, pick up a paint brush.

- Be a friend, be a volunteer "grandparent," offer to drive someone to the market, watch your neighbor's dog.

- Never quit learning—go back to school, read voraciously, explore new ideas.

- And last but not least, be productive! Get up, get out and DO something.

A few years ago I met a very remarkable lady who wears me out just talking about what she does to stay active. In her early 70s, she is a practicing massage therapist, she sells skin care products, she is a former lady Marine and is very active in that organization. She volunteers for just about everything. She's active in the local Kiwanis club, and she drives all over town visiting the elderly who are unable to get out. Mention retirement to her and she responds with, "Them's fighting words."

It is not the years in your life but the life in your years that count.
                                                           - Adlai Stevenson

---

Suzy Allegra, my friend and fellow author[1], talks about the belief in "youth is king," about how millions of advertising dollars push the idea of younger, thinner, better. Whatever happened to older, wiser, and perhaps, happier? Happier in our acceptance of ourselves, of our ability to say, "Been there, done that."

I believe we boomers have enough buying power, enough voting power, and enough vocal power to change that "youth is king" mentality. I refuse to believe that 76 million not-so-young, not-so-thin, and not-so-agile people will take this sitting down for very long.

---

[1] Suzy Allegra is the author of *How to Be Ageless, Growing Better, Not Just Older!*

A Boomer's Guide: Are You Ready for Retirement?

What looms for boomers: aging baby boomers say they won't settle for shuffleboard, bingo and early-bird dinners. They want second careers, exotic locales and the freedom to do their own thing. Chances are, they'll get it.

It was, at first, merely amusing. Picture America's 76 million bundles of post-World War II joy, the kids collectively called the baby boom, with pot bellies and gray hair — whatever's left, anyway — tottering off to apply for Social Security.

Now, with little more than 600 Mondays left in the oldest boomers' work lives, the prospect is more sobering. The generation that changed America in the '60s is certain to change it again as they enter their own 60s.

"Exactly how?" is a multi-billion dollar question.

The most fawned-over consumers in history are being asked again and again what they'd like to do, where they'd like to live and how they want to be treated in their leisure years. Just how leisurely those years will be remains to be seen. One survey found that eight in 10 boomers intend to keep working; others show similar results.

"The leading-edge baby boomers are likely to work at least 20 hours a week," says Charles F. Longino, Jr.., professor of gerontology at Wake Forest University in North Carolina. "They'll be returning for second careers. They'll be going back to school."

So much for bingo.

Longino, who has made a continuing study of retirement trends, is one of many who see the boomers headed for an oxymoronic future: active retirement. Some will work to pay the bills; others to keep from climbing the walls. After packing more rest-and-recreation time into their working lives than any generation in history, they'll be more inclined toward surfboards than shuffleboard—and less inclined to stay put.

"This has been a very mobile generation," Longino says.

Unlike the last-generation pioneers of Century Village, a local retirement community, some will be more adventurous in picking out-of-the-way destinations, from the once-rural American South to jungle-fringed beaches of South America. They'll be every bit as demanding, but they'll demand features foreign to most of today's retirement homes.

Del Webb Corp., the Arizona-based retirement builder, surveyed boomers across the nation last year and found that nearly 60 percent would rather have a gourmet kitchen than a swimming pool; most men (and many women) want a home office; and more than half want a house at least as big as the one they live in now.

Whatever they want, the boomers are likely to get it. Instead of being wheeled—or pushed—Boomer retirees will strut into their later years with a whole new attitude: Louder, more assertive, more engaged in the world around them. "They'll have the tools to make choices no one had before," says John Rother, legislative director of AARP. "They're more highly educated than today's retirees. They'll bring more economic clout." That will translate into unprecedented freedom to custom-design their own balance of work and play. "You're going to see a whole range of activities as people mix and match according to their own interests," Rother says. "More of them will be able to do their own thing, which is what boomers always wanted."

Making mass predictions about boomers isn't easy because they aren't one mass, just the coincidental by-products of postwar prosperity and pent-up passions. The label covers everyone born between 1946 and 1964.

"This is the most diverse generation in history," Rother says. "It is economically diverse. It is ethnically diverse. There's also considerable diversity of attitudes in men and women." The age spread creates its own diversity: The oldest were born before most Americans owned a television. The youngest were born after President Kennedy was assassinated.

America's over-60 population of boomers' parents and grandparents is already bigger than ever, at more than 30 million. Many will still be going strong when the boomers push the over-60 figure to 50 million by 2015. Late arrivals will bring the swell to full strength in 2030 at 65 million. By that time, the boomers who rocked Woodstock and protested Vietnam will be in their 80s, while the ones who grew up with the Brady Bunch will still have to show IDs to get into senior citizen buffet night.

Ray Hunter, senior vice president of ACTS Retirement Communities, is looking that far ahead. "Somebody described the boomers as a pig in a python," he says. "You can see them coming. They outnumber the generation before and the generation after. You have to start preparing now."

Hunter's non-profit communities, most in Florida and Pennsylvania, offer a mix of independent housing and various levels of assisted living, including nursing homes. They are sedate, dignified places that appeal mostly to people in their 80s. Hunter is trying to ensure that they will appeal to boomers in their 80s. Many communities are adding fitness centers, massage therapists and casual dining rooms with no dress code.

Hunter's already seeing generational friction. "Older residents don't want those things," he says. "They're happy the way things are. They don't like change."

The change no generation wants is the one no one can avoid: frailty, and the accompanying health problems of old age. Boomers have already done more than any generation to push it all back. They smoke less, eat more intelligently and some, at least, make an effort to stay fit. Eventually, though, they will have to make decisions about long-term care. Much sooner, they will have to make individual as well as public policy choices about how to pay for health care.

"The cost of health care has been going up at twice the rate of inflation for nearly 20 years," says the AARP's Rother. "It's the wild card in the Boomer's retirement. Your assets could disappear quickly if you've got to take a pill that costs $20 a day for the rest of your life."

There are other wild cards: The economy in general, the stock market—and how it reacts when boomers start pulling money out—plus whatever changes are to come in Social Security. (One change already suggests a rude surprise: Most boomers don't realize Congress raised their retirement age. Unlike their parents, who could collect full Social Security benefits at 65, the oldest boomers will have to wait until they're 66. The youngest will have to wait until age 67.) But barring big-picture disaster, as retirement nears, many boomers may be in better financial shape than their parents were. While often castigated as spenders rather than savers, they'll benefit from advantages that many in previous generations missed: employer-subsidized stock plans, IRAs and considerable equity in their homes. Some, however, won't be as lucky.

Up to a third of boomers, including many women and minorities, don't have pensions or health insurance, Rother says. "A lot of divorced women haven't saved for retirement," he says. "Unless something changes, they'll arrive at 65 with very few options except to continue working."

Some boomers may think they're in better shape than they really are. An annual survey released in May showed that most have some sort of retirement strategy or retirement savings and that more Americans than ever are very confident of having enough money to last to the end of their lives. The same survey showed that most thought they'd need to save only $50,000, that almost a quarter of all workers had actually saved less than $10,000 and that many were underestimating their expected life spans by 10 years or more.

Worse: Two out of 10 boomers hadn't begun to save at all.

"Yes, there are signs that some of the confidence may be misplaced," says Danny Devine of the Employee Benefit Research Institute, a Washington think tank that conducts the annual survey along with the affiliated non-profit American Savings Education Council. Still, Devine says the good omens in the survey outweigh the bad. "More people are paying attention to retirement," he says. "They're beginning to understand that they have to make a plan. They're taking small steps. Confidence comes from doing that."

Source: Douglas Kalajian, Palm Beach Post (West Palm Beach, FL) Publication Date: July 2, 2000, pp. "Reprinted by permission from the Post, West Palm Beach, Florida."

Common Sense Financial Planning

Just because your second cousin's son-in-law sells life insurance doesn't mean he is the best financial planner for you. Do not let family, friends, or co-workers be your resource for the care and feeding of your life savings.

Use common sense, research and interview techniques to determine the best financial advisor for you. And remember, who is best today may not be best in five years. Your money is your most important asset and annual reviews of your assets are not only advisable, they should be mandatory.

If you are looking for a financial planner, consider asking each one you interview the following questions:

1. What credentials do you have to practice financial planning?

    Financial planners come from a variety of backgrounds and, therefore, may hold a variety of degrees and licenses. There are no regulations in most states for the financial planning industry. However, some take specialized training in financial planning and earn credentials such as Certified Financial Planner (CFP) or Chartered Financial Consultant (ChFC). Others may hold degrees or registrations such as lawyer (JD), Certified Public Accountant (CPA), or Chartered Life Underwriter (CLU). Question financial planners carefully about their background and experience. Be certain that any planner you consider hiring has ample knowledge of taxes, insurance, estate and retirement planning issues, as well as the basics of investments and family budgeting.

    Be wary of individuals who promote various investment items without discussing any overall financial planning goal. They may lack the expertise to formulate one or they may be focusing solely on selling particular investments.

2. Are you registered with the federal Securities and Exchange Commission (SEC) or with a state agency?

   Anyone who may be giving advice on securities (including tax shelters), use of the stock market, or the value of securities over other types of investments should be registered with the SEC or registered under state law dealing with investment advisors.

3. How would you prepare my financial plan?

   Financial planners usually prepare financial plans after carefully discussing and analyzing your personal and financial history, your current situation, and your future goals. Some financial planners enter relevant financial information into a computer to generate standard financial plans. This type of plan may be useful, but be certain your unique financial situation is taken into account. Be sure to find an advisor who will give you personalized advice for your situation. Ask if you will be given a written analysis of your financial status and the planner's written recommendations to meet your goals.

   Also, ask the planner about the process for handling your account while you travel or, if for some reason, you cannot be reached. For example, if you give planners discretionary power over your account, they may buy and sell securities without your prior knowledge or approval. Discretionary authority is legal only when it is in writing. If you choose to give this power to your planner, be sure you and your planner agree exactly what action you want the planner to take. To revoke this discretionary permission, send a certified mail, return receipt letter to the planner. Be extremely careful about handing over this power to a planner. Many complaints to regulatory agencies about planners have to do with their misuse of discretionary power. And, be sure the planner is bonded. This insurance should protect you in case of fraud.

4. How many companies do you represent?

Someone who represents only one or two companies is probably not a financial planner, but a broker or salesperson. It will be to their advantage to see you purchase only those products offered by the companies they represent. You may want to seek an advisor who can offer you a wide range of choices to suit your needs. A fee-only planner does not represent any company.

5. Who will I work with on a regular basis?

You will want to work consistently with someone who is familiar with your account. If you work with a large firm offering many financial services, ask how the firm will provide a coordinated method of referral among the various experts who advise you. If you work with an individual planner, ask if the planner will provide you with professional references.

6. How do you keep up with the latest financial developments?

You may want to look for a planner who enrolls in continuing education courses to keep current on tax and investment strategies. Regular members of the National Association of Personal Financial Advisers (NAPFA) and the Institute of Certified Financial Planners (ICFP), for example, are required to complete 30 hours of continuing education every year in order to maintain full membership status.

7. Will you be involved in evaluating and updating the plan you suggest?

Financial planners should develop a plan specifically tailored to your situation and needs. Some planners also will include provisions for updating your plan to adjust to changes in your life, current economic conditions, and tax laws. A financial planner also can periodically review your plan to show you the progress being made in reaching your goals. Some planners offer continuous advice and management of your investments. Ask if your planner provides this type of ongoing service and what those services would cost.

8. Will you provide me with references?

   Ask for references of clients who have at least three years' experience with the planner. Talk to several. Ask these clients what they would most like to improve about their relationship with the planner.

9. Will you report the overall rates of return from all my investments so I can easily monitor results?

   Ask for a copy of this report for similar clients over the last five years (leaving the names of clients blank). Be careful not to compare stocks to CDs or stocks to bonds. To assess the impact of the planner's compensation on your investment results, be sure to ask for rates of return for before and after the deduction of the planner's compensation.

Source: AgeNet, LLC, © 1996, 1997, 1998, 1999. AgeNet is a registered trademark of AgeNet, LLC.

Considerations for a Divorced Person

Obviously, a divorce is not something you can plan for. However, if it is something you are considering, you should be sure to think about the financial implications of any decision you make regarding your settlement. Here are the financially related issues couples are faced with when ending a marriage.

1. **The house** – Three options for your house include: 1) selling and dividing the proceeds, 2) one spouse buying the other's share, 3) making a joint ownership agreement. You should weigh the pros and cons of each option carefully before making a decision.

2. **The value of your property** – The three basic questions you need to sort out are: 1) What is owned by you, your husband, or both of you jointly? 2) How much is the property worth? 3) How should you divide the property? Be sure to include any business interests you hold jointly.

3. **A qualified retirement plan or pension** – Retirement plans are considered to be joint property. There are two ways to divide a plan: 1) a buyout (cash out), when the non-employee spouse gets a lump-sum payout and the employee retains full interest in the remainder of the plan and 2) a deferred division (future share) when the value of the plan is determined and divided only when paid out by the plan. A Qualified Domestic Relations Order (QDRO) is the legal document used to inform the plan administrator of the agreement you've chosen regarding the plan assets.

> RESOURCE TIP:
> *Divorce Online*
> *www.divorceonline.com*
>
> *DivorceNet*
> *www.divorcenet.com*

4. **Alimony** – The three types of alimony arrangements are modifiable (if circumstances change, the alimony can be adjusted), non-modifiable (the arrangement is agreed upon at the time of the divorce and does not change), and rehabilitative (temporary payments are made until the spouse can support him/herself). Arrangements are based on need, ability to pay, length of marriage, maintaining pre-divorce standard of living, and the age and health of each spouse. Payments are taxable for the recipient and deductible by the payor.

5. **Child support** – State guidelines help courts decide levels of child support. Support payments are not taxable to the custodial parent and not deductible by the payor.

6. **Social Security benefits** – The lower-earning ex-spouse may be entitled to half of the other ex-spouse's benefits under certain conditions. Check with your local Social Security office or visit its Web site at www.ssa.gov.

7. **Insurance** – The three main types of insurance to think about are life, disability, and health. The ex-spouse may be named beneficiary of a life or disability policy in lieu of alimony. By law, an ex-spouse must continue to receive health insurance benefits as part of his or her ex-spouse's employer-sponsored plan.

8. **Debt** – Couples are jointly responsible for any debt incurred during a marriage. It's a good idea to pay off as much debt as possible before the divorce proceedings.

Source: MFG Investment Management's *"Life Planning: A Program for Women"* planner.

Qualified Domestic Relations Order (QDRO) Questions and Common Errors

Some questions to ask retirement plan administrators include:

❑ What if the employee dies before the start of benefit payments? What are the survivor benefits?

❑ Will the plan(s) split the account(s) on or after retirement?

❑ What is a spouse's claim if the employee doesn't retire?

❑ Will the plan pay out in a lump sum? Does it have to be annuitized?

❑ How does the plan handle QDROs?

Some common QDRO errors to avoid include:

❑ Failing to plan for the death of a spouse

❑ Not understanding retirement plan provisions and features

❑ Finalizing the divorce before the QDRO is approved by the plan

❑ Relying only on forms provided by the plan

❑ Failing to plan for a division of any early retirement bonus

❑ Not having the QDRO pre-approved by the plan administrator

Source: MFG Investment Management's *"Life Planning: A Program for Women"* planner.

Chapter 3

Now That I Have It,
Where Do I Keep It?

If you have built castles in the air, your work need not be lost; that is where they should be. Now put the foundations under them.
                                                                            - Henry David Thoreau

Now that we've talked about what we need, let's talk about what to do with it after we get it.

At the end of this chapter, you will find a list of important family documents. These are the basic documents that you and your family need to have. Your family will need to know where they are, and you will need to make sure they are in a safe, but easily accessible place. This list is the foundation for the following discussion.

It is important that you have your immediate family's records in some sense of order, and if you are a caregiver for an elderly loved one (parent, in-law, relative), you need to have documents for them as well. There is no way I could provide you with an all-encompassing list of every document you may have. However, it is my intent to provide you with a list of the very minimums you should have.

These documents should be readily accessible in case of emergency, but not necessarily kept all in one place. For example, you would not want your medical powers of attorney kept in the same location as your will. A member of your family may need to invoke a power of attorney on your behalf; but that does not mean this family member has the right to look at your will while you are living.

A few years ago when Mom came to live with me, I created a binder for each of us. All of our information has been written down in the binder and the documentation, if it will fit, has been placed in the slip sheets behind each page. We both know where these binders are kept and our trustee also knows of their existence and location.

At some point, Mom may have a medical emergency. If that should happen, I know exactly where her binder is. It contains her living will, her powers of attorney, her medical directives as well as her medical history, her insurance information, birth certificate, and copies of her insurance and social security cards and her driver's license/identification card. The hospital is going to want a lot of this information and I can save time and confusion by having it readily available. If we have a fire in our home, I may only have time to grab a couple of things – these organizers are the first things on my list.

Appendix D is an example of a Personal Papers Organizer. This Organizer has also been reproduced on a CD enclosed at the back of this book. Print out a copy of this organizer for you and your family members and start creating your own organizer.

> If I had a major emergency, would someone know where to find my documentation, prove they had Power of Attorney to make decisions for me, or provide proof of insurance? Who have I asked to assume this responsibility? _____
>
> _____
>
> _____

Everything does not need to be in one place. But everything should be listed and its location noted. A safety deposit box is a good secure storage place. However, make sure someone you trust – a family member, your attorney, whomever, knows where that box is located and also where you keep the key. And UNDER NO CIRCUMSTANCES should you ever put insurance policies in a safe deposit box.

Why do I say that? Do you know that most states secure bank accounts and safety deposit boxes as soon as they learn of the death of an account holder? While this is primarily so the tax man may get his due, it certainly puts a kink in your budget and your ability to move forward. When my father passed in 1969, we had to borrow the money from my aunt to bury him because Mom could not access their joint checking account.

There's one final item that needs to be mentioned when talking about where we keep our family records. As our personal lives increasingly go digital, family members, estate attorneys and online service providers are grappling more with what happens to those information bits when their owners die. It may be just e-mail messages, but sometimes it is financial records stored on a password-protected computer.

The computer is a great place for organizing, consolidating and maintaining information, however, if something should happen to us, does anyone know how to access this information? Privacy issues are in the news every day and online service providers are rightfully nervous about the subject. As more of our lives go online, we want to think carefully about the disposition of this information.

Considerations need to be given to this information when preparing your plan. When one family member tells another where the important paperwork is, the will, safe deposit box key, etc., the list of passwords should be added to it.

Basic Family Paperwork

Will and/or Trust Paperwork

Family Charitable Trust or Foundation Paperwork

Powers of Attorney

- Durable Power of Attorney – for financial matters[1]
- Health Care Powers of Attorney – needs to include a Mental Health Power of Attorney which could be a separate document

Living Will and Do Not Resuscitate Orders[2]

Other Health Care Directives

Identification Documents

- Marriage Licenses/Certificates
- Divorce Decrees
- Adoption Decrees
- Birth Certificates
- Death Certificates
- Social Security Cards
- Insurance ID Cards

Veterans/Military Paperwork, i.e., discharge papers and benefits information

Insurance Policies

- Life
- Long-Term Care
- Supplemental, i.e., cancer, long-term disability, intensive care
- Auto, Home and Other Property Policies

---

[1] For financial decisions – durable because it is still effective even during periods of incapacity

[2] At end of life stage, the living will supersedes the health care power of attorney.

Outstanding Promissory Notes
Vehicle Titles and Registrations
Bills of Sale
Property Deeds and Mortgage Papers
Credit Card Information – card numbers, name of card holders,
phone number of card company
Records of Investments including:
- Stocks and Bonds
- 401(k)s, IRAs
- CDs
- Mutual Funds

Banking information
- Checking and Savings Accounts
- Credit Union Accounts
- Safety Deposit Box Information (including where the key is kept)

Employment Related Paperwork
- Health Insurance Information
- Retirement/Pension Plan Paperwork
- Employer Provided Life Insurance

Prepaid Funeral Plans and Other Documentation
Tax Records
Warranties and Guarantees
A List of Your Advisors
- Accountant/CPA
- Financial Planner(s)/Investment Advisor(s)
- Attorney
- Primary Care Physician
- Other Medical Specialists
- Spiritual Advisors

Medical Records for each member of your family
- Medical History
- Allergies/Immunizations/Special Needs List

Chapter 4

Who Will Be Me for Me?

Have you ever asked yourself, "Who will be me for me?" What does that question mean to you? If you are like thousands of people in this country, at some point in your life, it will become a fundamental issue.

This is a very personal subject for me because Mother shares my home. As she goes through the aging process we are experiencing a reversal in roles. While she's in good health for her age, she's losing her independence. As mentioned in Chapter 1, she's no longer able to drive, uses a walker for mobility, has to wear hearing aids and glasses.

As more of my time is spent scheduling and taking her to doctor's appointments, the hair salon, and on shopping trips, it's always in the back of my mind who will do this for me when I reach her age? I have chosen the single lifestyle, have no children, and have led somewhat of a gypsy life. But as I progress along my own path of aging, I find myself talking with my friends, most of whom are my age or older, about the various challenges of aging. It's easy now to say we'll be there for each other, but when we are all in our 80s that may be a problem. And, this subject isn't just for singles.

Our parents never dreamed they'd be living with, or dependent upon, their kids, but they have always believed that their offspring would make sure their needs were met. We baby boomers don't have that reassurance. Even those of us with children must consider how our kids will accept the responsibility and how they will handle the problems associated with aging parents. In a time of crisis, if the kids live across the country, who will make the immediate and critical decisions for us? We need to think about what we want, who will ensure that our wishes are carried out and how we are going to pay for it.

What about our personal support group? Do we have younger friends? What are the ages of our physicians and other health care providers? Can we be sure that those people will be around when we need them? Are there any easy answers? No, there are not. Do we need to start thinking about all that is involved? Yes, we do.

> Have I ever thought about these things and do they concern me?
>
> ❏ Yes   ❏ No
>
> If yes, what conclusions have I reached? If no, when will I?
>
> _____
>
> _____
>
> _____

Growing old is no gradual decline, but a series of tumbles, full of sorrow, from one ledge to another. Yet when we pick ourselves up, we find that our bones are not broken; while not unpleasing is the new terrace which lies unexplored before us.

- Logan Pearsall Smith (1856-1946), US Humorist

Some of us remember the sad story of Doris Duke, the heiress to the American Tobacco Company. A shrewd money manager and investor, she parlayed her $30 million dollar inheritance into a massive $750 million dollar fortune. She lived a life most of us only dream of, traveling all over the world and socializing with the rich and famous. She was also an environmentalist and animal rights advocate, with several homes across the continents.

She never had children and as she grew older she trusted employees who proved to be less than trustworthy. During the last years of her life, her butler successfully cut her off from what few relatives she had, essentially isolating her from the rest of the world. She named her butler co-executor of her will and it was rumored that he lent a hand to her demise. Although nothing was ever proven, he was given a substantial amount of money to remove himself from the management of her estate and died three years later.

If you have no family, is this what you want to happen to you? Perhaps you don't have millions, but can you trust the person who has been tasked with managing what funds you do have?

Do you have adequate long-term care insurance, or sufficient funds to pay for private care? ❑ Yes ❑ No

Do you have sufficient savings to pay for your housing and your care when the time comes? ❑ Yes ❑ No

Do you know what the average monthly cost for assisted living is today? ❑ Yes ❑ No
If so, and you think it's high now, just wait another 20 years. Cost may not be the primary issue; it may be availability.

There is an ever increasing shortage of health care providers and those who are in the business are leaving because of low wages and poor working conditions. Today, the average age of a caregiver is 40. Thirty years from now are we going to be a society of poverty stricken seniors only minutes away from eviction and starvation? Will Social Security and Medicare programs have adequate funding when it's your turn to draw on them? We are going to have to take care of ourselves and view public-funded programs as a "bonus" if and when available and if we can qualify. And, as the aging population grows, even our customary support organizations such as our churches and community senior centers may no longer be able to keep up with the demand.

And it isn't all financial. Who will be your spokesperson if you are unable to speak for yourself? Who will purchase and deliver your groceries and other necessities of life, make sure your medications are taken on time and as directed, and most of all, who will be there for just a friendly chat or to take you out to dinner and a movie every once in a while? Isolation, loneliness and depression are major factors in an aging population, so perhaps communal living is an option you could consider.

Many studies have found that strong friendships reduce the risk for disease by lowering blood pressure, heart rate, and cholesterol. Research indicates that children in positive friendships are less prone to bullying, adult friendships reduce stress and anxiety and provide courage and support, and that friendships are a buffer against loneliness and depression for older adults. The more friends women had, the less likely they were to develop physical impairments.[1]

Below are some helpful hints on developing friendships and maintaining them.

Finding New Friends
- Be a people person
- Find new friends through activities you enjoy
- Join a support group
- Attend community activities
- Volunteer
- Make friends of acquaintances
- Think quality, not quantity

Being a Friend
- Be a good listener
- Keep personal information confidential
- Have a good time
- Stay in touch

[1] Source: Vitality magazine, July 2004 edition, by Barbara Floria, editor.

Outside of my family, who can I count on in a time of need? Who are my closest friends and are we ready, willing and able to help each other when called upon? And are they of various ages?

_____

_____

_____

_____

On a personal level, what can we do now to start the process of taking care of ourselves? Seek out the absolute best long-term care insurance you can find for your own particular situation. Make sure your physicians and health care providers know, and have written instructions about what you want and how you want it. Make sure your legal affairs are in order. Are your investments safe and do you feel secure that they will remain so? Do you trust your financial advisor? Who holds your powers of attorney? If it's a friend, or even a distant relative, will they absolutely abide by your wishes, or will they try to insert their own beliefs into your life? Who will pay your bills on time when you can no longer handle your own finances?

On a grander scale, are you concerned enough to start taking action? Would you consider organizing a grass roots coalition within your community to address these issues and seek solutions? Perhaps we need to revisit the days of old when we had real "neighborhoods" where everyone looked out for everyone else. Would you be willing to volunteer time if programs were in place? What are you willing to do today to ensure your future lifestyle remains the same? We baby boomers have a tremendous opportunity to make some very important changes in the mindset of our peers and our children Are we willing to step up to the plate?

Is Communal Living Back in our Future?

The friends-helping-friends model for aging is gaining momentum among single, widowed or divorced women of a certain age. The logic is compelling. Baby boomer women, many of whom have managed businesses or owned real estate, are accustomed to controlling their own lives. They tend to have close female friendships. Many have watched the slow death of their parents, dependent on children or paid caretakers. They want something better for themselves. Aging with friends could be the answer.

Recently, I read an article about two women who had been friends since childhood. Both widows, they were discussing the idea of sharing a home in their later years. One of them said, "We've already shared the good and bad for over 60 years. There would be no surprises. We know how to care for each other because we know how to care for ourselves. All we want is to safeguard our quality of life, our independence and our pride."

Taking care of our own parents, an experience of growing numbers of baby boomers, has been "a wake-up call" Especially when we have no children, our fears quicken. Another lady, who spent down her retirement savings caring for her mother after she broke a hip, wondered, "What in the name of God will become of me?" But her worries eased when she and five women friends in the same town visualized their future in a rural setting. One of them inherited a farm where these half-dozen women already vacation together. With outbuildings that could be upgraded for live-in caregivers, and with a pottery studio and a view of the mountains, "It would not be a bad way to complete our lives," one of them said.

Women seem to be drawn to this idea not only because they expect to outlive their mates but also because they trust their friends to be good caretakers. One of these six was married for 25 years, was on her own for 10 years and is now with a male partner she describes as totally reliable. Still, she prefers the idea of aging with friends. "A lot of men just can't go there," she said. "They didn't change their children's diapers, so why do we think they're going to change their wives'?"

Men do not seem to entertain comparable ideas. Dennis Kodner, executive director of the Brookdale Center on Aging, at Hunter College, says all the men he knows expect that a woman will care for them. "We don't really have those kinds of friendships," Mr. Kodner said.

But what about the legalities? Especially if one woman has children or other family members and one does not? Who gets the house when one passes? Some states now allow for beneficiary deeds to enable property to pass much like life insurance or annuities with beneficiary designations. Perhaps this is where we are headed when there will be so many of us. Medically, it's been proven that we live healthier lives in the company of others versus living in isolation. It's certainly much more pleasant to have someone to eat dinner with than to eat alone.

These are issues that we need to start considering now, before it's too late. Let's get the legal and financial problems handled so that we "old women" may live out our lives in relative peace and comfort in the company of good friends.

Many boomers May Face Old Age All Alone

Nancy Sheaffer says she will count on God, an extended church family and the kindness of strangers to do for her what she is doing for her 80-year-old mother, Bonnie Lynch: provide care in old age. That's because neither she nor her second husband has children. Her mother, in good health but having "up and down days," lives with them in Richmond, Va. "If I end up in a home," says Sheaffer, 44, "that's the way it goes. I go back to my belief that I will be taken care of when I need to be." She is probably more trusting than most of her Boomer generation when it comes to answering the question, "Who will take care of me?"

In an aging America, with increasingly fragmented families and the potential for record numbers needing care, most experts say elder care is a crisis in waiting. Millions of baby boomers could be left with no one around to tend to them when they are old and frail. The combination of factors will make tomorrow's "caregiving burden the single most devastating social, economic and spiritual sinkhole of the early decades of the 21st century," says Ken Dychtwald, a psychologist, gerontologist and author of "Age Power." "It could be a death blow to our thriving culture and economy."

Experts see a convergence of long-term trends:

America's population is aging. The leading edge of the 78 million baby boomers – those born between 1946 and 1964 – are heading toward retirement and becoming the "young old." According to the Census Bureau, the number of people ages 65 to 74 will grow 107 percent by 2030.

Boomers have fewer children than their parents, leaving a shortage of adult children to act as caregivers down the line. Like Sheaffer, almost one-fifth (19 percent) of women in their early 40s have no children.

Boomers will live longer. The life expectancy for a person born in 1957 – the peak of the baby boom – was about 70 years at birth, according to the National Center for Health Statistics. That's six to 15 years longer than their parents' generation. A huge number will reach an age requiring assistance at the same time, choking the already gasping caregiving system.

The concept of "family" has changed, creating a powerful societal shift that will alter the face of caregiving. boomers have chosen to divorce, to cohabit, to remarry and create stepfamilies, to remain single, to marry and not have children. Mounting research shows that divorce and blended families tend to weaken ties between generations. Most at risk are divorced dads who have lost close touch with their children.

Experts are just beginning to study the effects today's restructured families will have on care giving. So far, they find few answers.

Carol Dawson worries about her 14-year-old son's generation. "These kids have several sets of grandparents," from various step and blood relationships, says Dawson, 44, of Jeffersonville, Ind. "My son will have a mom, a dad, a stepdad and, maybe down the road, a stepmom. These kids will have huge responsibilities."

Boomers just have not done much thinking about their future need for elder care, says Jake Sheaffer, 42, Nancy's husband. "And that is really scary. We live in an increasingly complicated world. The Ozzie-and-Harriet family is pretty much passé." People in their 80s – the old old – are most likely to fall ill and to need care. And their numbers will burgeon. By 2020, 7 million people will be 85 or older, says the National Institute on Aging. That group will at least double again by 2040.

Although those boomers will live longer than their parents, the prognosis is mixed. Demographer Kenneth Wachter of the University of California at Berkeley, thinks technological advances will lead to fewer people with disabilities among the frail elderly.

But others worry about the future health picture. "The probability that someone will get dementia, Alzheimer's and stroke-related diseases rises dramatically during one's 80s," says Robert Willis of the Institute for Social Research at the University of Michigan. "As other causes of disease decline, it is more likely people will end their lives in a demented state." The Alzheimer's Association says 4 million Americans have the disease now. Without a cure, that number is expected to jump to 14 million by 2050. The reassembling of families – through divorce, remarriage and cohabitation – is prompting a hot debate: Will the divorced and remarried receive the same support from adult children, particularly stepchildren, as those who stayed in intact families?

Demographer Wachter has developed projections sponsored by the National Institute on Aging and published in the British Royal Society journal "Philosophical Transactions: Biological Sciences":

Stepchildren. People who are now 70 to 85 have an average of 2.5 living biological children. But that age group in 2030 will have an average of 1.5 children. The mix changes if you add in stepchildren, whose numbers could help make up for the loss.

Stepgrandchildren. The number of biological grandchildren will drop by 40 percent for 70- to 85-year-olds, from four grandchildren today to 2.5 in 2030. But the average goes back up to four in 2030 if stepgrandchildren are added in.

Wachter believes the "steps" will step up to the plate and provide elder care, although they do not tend to do so now. In the future, he believes, there will be so many of them that being "stepkin will be commonplace and somewhat normal." The health care system will be so stressed that stepkin will see that "the need is stronger."

Elizabeth Bier Krieg thinks her kids will be there for her. She has one child from her first marriage, two from her second, and a stepson from her third. "I have no doubt when I become old, my children will watch over me. They will get together and provide a solution," says Krieg, 47, of Bethel, Vt.

But there is a growing body of research that says expanded families can't be counted on later in life when the going gets tough. The elderly may be able to rely on the expanded step network "for an occasional dinner or symphony ticket," says researcher Lynn White of the University of Nebraska-Lincoln.

"But the network will not be there to help you go to the toilet."

Divorce itself increases the risk that the aging parent's adult children will not be there when needed, experts say. "If parents do not stay involved with their kids after divorce, the kids are often not in the picture for those parents when they need help," says Lawrence Ganong, a University of Missouri-Columbia researcher and co-author of "Changing Families, Changing Responsibilities." "Genetic ties do not matter as much as the quality of the relationship between the generations."

Aging single moms will get support from their adult children as long as the moms stay single, but the help dwindles if the moms remarry, says sociologist Paul Amato of Pennsylvania State University. And biological children are much more likely to help their moms than stepchildren are to rally for their stepmoms, says Beth Soldo of the University of Pennsylvania.

Sally Corwin-Osgood of the Stepfamily Association of America knows how second marriages can compound the complications of caregiving. She gave up her career as a nurse and moved 900 miles with her second husband and her child to provide substantial elder care for her mother-in-law. "The remarriage factor certainly complicates being a daughter-in-law," says Corwin-Osgood, 48, of Cleveland. "I came here to make caregiving a priority, and I still feel like an outsider in his family."

Most at risk for being left without help from adult children are divorced dads, many researchers say. Although custody arrangements are changing, the kids often go to Mom. "Perhaps half of divorced men are estranged from their children," White says. "There is liable to not be anybody around for them. On the other hand, they often remarry and will be taken care of by their younger wives," Amato says.

William Paprota, 49, of Overland Park, Kan., is a divorced dad whose children live with their mother in Salina, Kan. "Maybe I need to run out and get married," he says. Short of that, he works hard to keep up close relationships with his two daughters. "If you pay attention to your child, she will pay attention to you." He also has a sister nearby who is "single, with no children, and is a mother hen. And she is a dear friend." But Paprota, a divorce lawyer, agrees that divorced Boomer men may not be well cared for in later years. "It is more difficult for men to have intimate friends. When they get a divorce, they find themselves isolated, totally cut off."

Adding to the complex future of elder care are two trends, says Bonnie Lawrence of the Family Caregiver Alliance. Today's society is mobile, and divorce often causes families to move. "The long distance between families has a huge impact," Lawrence says. And although some surveys show that more men are providing elder care, women are the traditional caregivers. And "women now are in the workforce."

The caregiving, working women of today – and tomorrow – are part of the "sandwich generation," looking after their children and their parents. And in disrupted families, they often do it alone, a situation many of the boomers' children will face.

Joan Cooper, a divorced teacher, cared for her folks in her home while she still had two teen-agers living with her. With 13 other women, she wrote about the experience in "Fourteen Friends' Guide to Eldercaring." Cooper's mom is in a retirement facility now, but her father died in Cooper's home at 79. "He taught me the dignity of what it means to have to die," says Cooper, 56, of Dallas. She empathizes with the single caregivers of the future. "In the privacy of my bedroom, I wept. It is very lonely first of all to be a single adult, and even lonelier when you just have so much to take care of. You can't turn to someone."

Many boomers think caregiving will be made easier for restructured families in the future because their sheer numbers will demand solutions.

"I'm a Boomer, and we are not a quiet generation," says Suzanne Mintz of the National Family Caregivers Association. "There are no guarantees, but as we roll into that next phase, there will be answers."

Source: USA Today, by Karen S. Peterson and contributing: USA Today reporter Anthony DeBarros, Publication Date: Dec. 12, 2000, Copyright (c) GANNETT NEWS SERVICE, INC. and/or USA TODAY.

Chapter 5

The Challenges of a
Working Caregiver

Everything works out in the end. If it hasn't worked out, it's not the end.
                                                                    – Unknown

At some point each of us will most likely be caregivers to an elderly loved one. Forty percent of those caregivers are and will continue to be men. It's not just affecting employees, but management staff as well. And the problem of keeping the workforce focused on their job while at their job is a challenge for every human resources professional.

NOTE: Recent studies indicate that nearly one out of every four U.S. households (23% or 22.4 million households) is involved in caregiving and that nearly 7 million Americans provide long distance care to an elderly loved one. baby boomers, the "sandwich generation," are likely to spend more years caring for their parents than they did for their children.

So how can we focus on our job when we're wondering how Mom came through surgery? Or, has Dad taken his medication this morning? Or, is my mother-in-law able to live alone now that her husband is no longer with her?

Nationwide, we hear of people experiencing one or more of the following everyday:[1]

- An only son drives hundreds of miles every week to the next state to look in on his mother, spend an afternoon talking with

---

[1] Source: Dychwald, Ken, *Age Wave*, Bantam Books, 1990

her, take care of bills and arrange for the plumber, the insurance payments, and the social worker's visit.

- A family moves grandpa's daybed into the living room so that he can see and be seen most easily. The teenage children begin asking their friends not to drop by.

- A librarian drops out of her graduate studies so that she can spend every lunch hour and an hour each evening at the local convalescent home with her mother-in-law.

- A struggling couple pays for their parents' mounting health bills with their steadily depleting savings.

- A construction worker leaves work early two days each week to cook dinner for his father.

- Siblings argue over who will take care of Mom now that Dad has passed away.

In 1940, only 13 percent of people over 60 had a living parent. In 2000, 44 percent did. This chapter looks at how to deal with parents, in-laws and other relatives who may be in a state of transition due to aging. It may be an illness, memory loss, or nothing more than making sure you know what their wishes are and that you have made the proper arrangements to ensure that their wishes are granted.

As stated previously, my Mother and I have shared a home since 1994. Although she's in good health, we have gone through eye surgery, balance and stability problems, giving up her car and being hesitant about managing her checkbook. In almost every sense of the word, I am a full-time caregiver.

Mom and I have a very unique relationship as she's willingly shared with me all of her personal information. When consulting with clients, I've found that isn't always the case. Experience has shown that by using humor and a little reverse psychology, sometimes we can get to those details and make suggestions that will give us much of the information we are looking for to ensure their wishes are met. If your loved one(s) live nearby, your job is much easier than if you are dealing with issues of distance as well as health and/or other problems associated with aging.

Long distance caregiving is difficult because of the distance and the guilt of not being there for your parent. She (Mom) was there for me when I was little. Will my kids be there for me?
- MetLife survey respondent

So what is the biggest concern of Mom or Dad? Most likely it will be, "I don't want to be a burden on anyone."

Therefore, they keep things to themselves, including changes in health, living conditions, and perhaps even a car accident. Reverse that "I'm a burden therefore I'm not going to tell" attitude by approaching the issue with, "Mom, I'm concerned about you (or whatever issue it may be). You know I work a full-time job and am trying to raise a family, and you'd be doing me a huge favor if you would....." It may be:

- "use a walker,"

- "try a home companion service for a couple of weeks,"

- "write down your health care professionals' names and contact information,"

- "give me limited power of attorney to act on your behalf if you become unable to speak for yourself."

The most important thing to remember when beginning a dialogue with your loved one is to listen. You must remember that this is about THEIR life; what they want — not what you think they want or should have and/or do.

It's extremely important that you involve the entire family (siblings, spouses, and anyone else directly involved) in the family meeting. Even though everyone is in agreement today, that doesn't ensure they will be tomorrow.

Consider this example:

> You live close to Mom and Dad and your siblings live out of state. Dad has some memory problems and Mom's health isn't good. You've talked with them about giving you Power of Attorney for financial and medical issues. Your siblings have said in the past that the decisions are yours to make. Mom goes into the hospital and you have to make some medical as well as financial decisions. Your sister finds out and raises questions. A family argument ensues and there is a rift. These kinds of instances can be avoided if a family meeting had been held and agreement reached prior to the need.

Remember to give your elder loved ones time to think things over, but do not let them procrastinate until it's too late. Plant the seeds today and let them take root, but make sure you nourish the seedling and harvest in a timely manner. While nagging isn't recommended, gentle reminders will serve you well in the long run.

And last but not least, you must remember it is their lives and ultimately the decisions should be theirs. Now that we're having a meeting, what do we need to discuss?

- Powers of attorney — both medical and financial

- Wills and/or trusts

- Funeral plans: What do they want and is it paid for?

- In-home care or assisted living facilities

- What are the financial conditions? Who pays for what?

- Where are their important papers? Life and long-term care insurance, burial plans, house deed and car titles, pension information, where is their bank, is there a safe deposit box?

All these little things become big things at a time of urgent need.

Your goal is for your loved one to understand that powers of attorney, legal directives and such are about what they want; not what you want. They need to understand what will happen if no directives are in place and they can't speak for themselves in an emergency. Let them know that you can't make a decision for them if you don't know what they want. For example, when Mom and I were talking about funeral planning, she told me she only wanted a graveside service. That really surprised me, as a church service is tradition in her family. When I questioned her, she said, "who would come? I've outlived all my family and friends except my two daughters and granddaughter."

Your family and your loved ones need to understand that you are trying to plan for an eventual need – that being prepared is better than making decisions during crisis when emotions take control over common sense. My consulting service focuses on helping to arrange and facilitate family meetings. Most have been very positive and agreement was reached in an atmosphere of caring and concern about what was best for their loved one. However, one comes to mind where three sisters and one brother were passionately disagreeing over Dad's funeral plan. Dad, who had been quietly observing his kids argue like children, banged his hand on the table and with great effort said, "Aren't you forgetting about what I want? I'm not dead yet!" Nothing I can think of will bring a discussion back into focus like that comment.

And last but certainly not least, I'd like to spend a few minutes on caregiver issues. As a full-time caregiver, I can truthfully say it has been a rewarding experience, but it can also be one of the most stressful jobs you'll ever do. Patience may be a virtue, but it comes with a price tag. Managing stress becomes one of the most important things you must do for yourself. Just remember, if you get down, then there are two of you requiring care.

Whether you're sharing a home with an elderly parent or just live nearby, you are responsible for their well-being. While they look to you to take care of them, they will at times treat you like a 5 year old. To them, you are still their child.

Some time ago, I attended a caregiver conference and Debbie Reynolds was the keynote speaker. From the age of 14, Debbie has been a caregiver to one or another family member, and she does this while retaining her marvelous sense of humor. Her advice? Be indifferent. You need thick skin and don't take it personally.

There's nothing like biting off more than you can chew, and then chewing it anyway.
                                                    - Mark Burnett

---

Your loved one will lash out at losing their independence, their health, their hearing and so forth. They aren't blaming you – but like you, they just need to vent and most times you are the most convenient receptacle.

You must take time for you. If you are stopping by Dad's house everyday and a short visit turns into several hours, there are things that aren't getting done in your life. Does he need to visit his doctor? Who takes him? Does Mom need groceries? If so, are you responsible for shopping? Are they eating nourishing meals if left alone – probably not. All these little things take you away from your job, your family and your life.

Consider hiring a non-medical home care company to help you out. Even if it's just to fix and share a meal at lunchtime, it will certainly ease your load. Go to the movies, go to the spa, or play a round of golf. Do whatever makes you feel good and don't feel guilty about it. I can't stress this enough.

Caregivers definitely gain a whole new appreciation for the phrase "Grumpy Old Men" (or women). Your loved one's number one fear is being a burden on anyone. So when you approach them with the idea of a companion service, relocating to an assisted living home, or the need to purchase and use a walker, approach the subject not as "I want you to…", but as "Mom, it would really help me a lot if you would consider…" This has never failed in my case. I tease Mom about being chronologically gifted and memory challenged, not about getting old. Using humor in communication can be very effective.

I am running myself ragged trying to take care of my grandmother and do a good job here at work. The only person I am shortchanging is myself.

- MetLife survey respondent

NOTE:

- Caregivers suffer more depression and illness than non-caregivers, stretching our healthcare system and dollars.

- Caregivers run a 63% greater risk of dying prematurely.

- Family caregivers account for an estimated $257 billion annually in services, if they were paid.

Stress Management - Perspectives and Values

A lecturer, when explaining stress management to an audience, raised a glass of water and asked, "How heavy is this glass of water?" Answers called out ranged from 20g to 500g. The lecturer replied, "The absolute weight doesn't matter. It depends on how long you try to hold it . If I hold it for a minute, that's not a problem. If I hold it for an hour, I'll have an ache in my right arm. If I hold it for a day, you'll have to call an ambulance. In each case, it's the same weight, but the longer I hold it, the heavier it becomes."

He continued, "And that's the way it is with stress management. If we carry our burdens all the time, sooner or later, as the burden becomes increasingly heavy, we won't be able to carry on. As with the glass of water, you have to put it down for a while and rest before holding it again. When we're refreshed, we can carry on with the burden."

So, before you return home tonight, put the burden of work down. Don't carry it home. You can pick it up tomorrow. Whatever burdens you're carrying now, put them down for a moment if you can. Relax; pick them up later after you've rested. Life is short. Enjoy it!

The following profile was taken from *The MetLife Study of Sons at Work, Balancing Employment and Eldercare.* Findings from a National Study by the National Alliance for Caregiving and The Center for Productive Aging at Towson University, June 2003.

A Profile of a Male Caregiver

The following profile reflects the characteristics of many of the men who responded to the survey:

Jim, a 48-year-old accountant working for a large international corporation, has been helping his mother for two years. His mother, now 79 years of age, relies upon Jim to help with a range of tasks including transportation to and from doctors' appointments, grocery shopping, housework and medication management. Jim also occasionally prepares meals for his mom.

Jim spends about 12 hours a week taking care of things for his mother. He stops by her apartment every other evening on his way home from work, checks on the home health aide during the day, and phones her to make sure that the "meals-on-wheels" driver has shown up. One thing that Jim has become acutely aware of during his two years as a caregiver is that just when he thinks the care arrangements are working smoothly, something will change and require his attention. The home health aide quits, his mother's health changes, or his mother's physician decides not to accept a Medicare assignment, requiring Jim to make other arrangements. It's a logistical and emotional roller coaster for Jim. He's grateful for the support of his wife who is there to pitch in when things get too complicated and takes too much time away from his work.

Jim has difficulty talking about his caregiving situation at work. He feels as if his boss might think he is not serious about his career if he brings his personal life into the office. And he does not want to talk to his co-workers about his problems—having heard their complaints about having to carry the load of other workers with family distractions. Fortunately, Jim's employer has a flextime policy that has made it possible for Jim to miss work during the middle of the day providing he has planned for his absence in advance. This policy doesn't require him to share his reason for the absence. Jim's employer also has an eldercare program that provides caregiving employees with information and linkages with eldercare services and with other support services. However, Jim was not aware of this program when we spoke with him. He thought the program sounded like a good idea, but wouldn't use it if he had to let any of his co-workers or supervisors know about it.

Although Jim believes that he has done a good job keeping his work and caregiving separate and managing them both, he is finding it increasingly difficult and is considering a job change. He feels as if there might be a new job for him in a company that allows him more flexibility in scheduling and where he doesn't need to travel. And he frankly is concerned that his mother's deteriorating health condition might require more work accommodations and revelations to his supervisor and co-workers about his situation.

Tips for Caregivers: Coping With Stress and Anxiety

Here are a few guidelines you can use now to help alleviate your anxiety.

- Recognize and admit that you are feeling stressed and anxious.

- Become aware of your body's symptoms. Don't let them scare you, let them talk to you.

- Try to pinpoint what it is you are anxious about. What happened yesterday? What were you thinking about before you went to bed? If you can't pinpoint it, don't worry about it and move on.

- Give yourself permission to feel anxious about whatever it is that is bothering you. "Of course, I feel anxious about this problem, anyone would. But how much anxiety is too much?"

If you do know what it is that is bothering you, what can you do to eliminate or minimize the situation in some way so that it isn't so stressful? Most importantly, how can you react differently, so you won't be so affected by this situation? Here are some things to think about:

- Listen to the dialogue within yourself. Are you filling yourself full of negative thoughts about a certain situation? What could you say to yourself that would feel more comforting?

- Listen to the dialogue of those around you. Is someone around you being negative and dragging you down with them? If so, how could you change your reaction to their negative attitude, so that you would be less affected by it?

- Are you overwhelming yourself with "shouldas" and high expectations? If so, which ones could you eliminate?

- Are you blaming someone else for your anxieties, unhappiness, poor health, lack of success, etc.? How can you take responsibility for yourself and make some positive changes?

- Give yourself positive reinforcement for even the smallest accomplishments.

No one lives a life without a certain amount of stress and anxiety. The key is to get the level of both down to a manageable level. Listening to your "inner voice" is a step in the right direction. You know best what you need.

The Accidental Caregiver
by Rev. Anton Grosz, HHA

Like most family members who find themselves called to serve, I became a caregiver quite by accident. In my case it was a driver at the airport whose foot slipped onto the accelerator as my wife, Phyllis, was taking luggage out of the back seat of our car. Suddenly, her vacation to visit our daughter and grandson cross country became a siren wailing trip to the hospital cross town and my planned week alone became a bedside vigil. When she was finally released from the hospital, I was a full-time caregiver.

Everybody's story of how they became a family caregiver is unique. An accident, an illness, an aging parent, a child or grandchild come into the world unable to live on their own. Does it really matter what the cause? A loved one is in need and we are there. After all, we tell ourselves, if we didn't do it, who would?

I was lucky. I had some idea of what I was getting into. Back a number of years ago when I was still trying to figure out what to do with my life, I used to visit an old blind friend, (younger than I am now) whose kidneys didn't work. We'd hang out and talk and I'd read him his favorite passages from the Bible, as well as excerpts from the book I was writing at the time.

"Ya know," Don said to me once as he was hooked up to the dialysis machine, "If ya wanna minister to men's souls, ya really oughta know how to minister to their bodies as well." It made sense, so I took a course, (I was the only man in it), and became a state certified Home Health Aide, HHA. I spent the next several years working with clients of all shapes, sizes, ages, and conditions until my back went out (a major hazard for caregivers) and I was forced to quit the profession. I still can't lift anything heavy.

However, that training and experience has come to my aid now, as I change dressings and safety proof our apartment, cook meals and wash laundry. As I do, I can't help thinking about those family caregivers who haven't been formally trained and who do what we do purely out of love and caring for the person who needs it, simply because it needs to be done. And that's why I thought I'd write this column and share some thoughts on this sacred work we find ourselves doing.

For make no bones about it, caregiving is sacred. Whatever your faith, whatever your beliefs, what greater service to humanity can there be than to care for someone who cannot care for themselves? "I was sick and ye visited me," said Jesus of Nazareth. "Inasmuch as ye have done it unto the least of these my brethren, ye have done it unto me." You are doing great works. Keep this in mind as you strive to keep going day after day in a job that can be not only hard, stressful, tiring, and demanding, but often frustrating and thankless.

A caregiver's work is most often done in private. There are no reporters, TV cameras, or admiring fans waiting in the wings to cheer us for a job well done. There is no one there to pump us up. We must be strong-willed and self-motivated in order to reach inside ourselves day after day to find the strength to continue.

Anton Grosz is an author of several books on end-of-life issues and Pastoral Counselor for TRANSITIONS, a San Francisco non-profit offering free counseling for the terminally ill, their families, and caregivers. The books are available through caregiver.com or by calling 1-800-829-2734. He can be reached at: ag@transitionssupport.org

Chapter 6

Defining the Generations

As we're talking about the challenges of working caregivers, living alone and longer, along with the increasing numbers of us that are flooding the system, we need to take a look at the events that have defined the generations and groups within those generations.

Who are these different generations and what are their characteristics?

Let's take a look at four generations and their characteristics so we may better understand what this chapter is all about. It can get pretty complex. Each generation is motivated differently, aspires to different personal and professional goals, and interprets just about everything in life in drastically diverse fashion. Four generations – four times the fun (and four times the challenge).

Following the defining characteristics of each of the four generations, the Matures, the Boomers, the Xers, and the Millennials, we will take a look at the defining decades from 1950 to 2000. In his *Boomer Nation: The Largest and Richest Generation Ever, and How It Changed America*, Steve Gillon talks about the Boomers as the biggest, righest generation and its impact on America. What an eye opener to learn that in 1959 there were as many children as there were total people living in the United States in 1881. Wow! That's a lot of people. The United States, and some say the world, has evolved as the Boomer generation has aged. And as Mr. Gillon states, "Though they pushed the country toward liberalism when they were young, they pushed it right back to conservatism when they grew older. Beneath all the contradictions, there is a strong signal: they have reshaped an entire culture around their own single cohort."

The Matures:

-   Born between: 1909 - 1945

-   When you think of this generation think: Duty, Sacrifice

-   Cost of living index: A 1942 dollar would buy $11.25 worth of goods today.

-   Popular toys: Doll babies, tin cars and trucks, wagons, homemade wooden toys, books.

-   Formative events:
    -   The Great Depression
    -   Pearl Harbor
    -   WWII
    -   Hiroshima

-   Think of:
    -   Jimmy Carter
    -   Charlton Heston
    -   John Glenn
    -   George Bush
    -   Billy Graham

They began their careers after World War II, when the premise was that the corporation rewards loyalty with loyalty back to you. They came of age when there were flush times for white men, scarce opportunities for others.

The Matures are actually a combination of two generations, the Veterans (1901 – 1924) and the Silent Generation (1925 – 1942), whose characteristics in the workplace are very similar. They either fought in World War II or were children during the war. The eldest members of the Matures remember the Great Depression and their memories of those times have made an indelible mark on them. Many of their behaviors today can be traced back to their experiences during the Depression.

Of the four generations, the Matures are the smallest in numbers (55 million). They're also the wealthiest. They either first entered the workforce after WWII or came home from the war and got a job with companies that took care of their employees. Both the company and the employee believed that loyalty to one another created even more loyalty. Most of the Matures worked for only one company in their lifetime and stayed with their employer until they retired and the company rewarded them with a gold watch. The post-war workplace they inhabited was primarily male dominated. The mothers stayed at home and kept the house and raised the children.

Today the Matures are being acknowledged on every front for their efforts. They're being written about by Tom Brokaw ("The Greatest Generation"), featured in films ("Saving Private Ryan," "Band of Brothers") and are courted by politicians since they vote en masse. They have one of the nation's most powerful lobbies in the AARP.

The Boomers:

- Born between: 1946 – 1964

- When you think of this generation think: Individuality, "Me" Generation

- Cost of living index: A 1966 dollar would buy $5.66 worth of goods today.

- Popular toys: Barbie dolls, Hula-Hoops, electric trains, Hot Wheels, sleds, bicycles.

- Formative events:
  - The Civil Rights Movement
  - John F. Kennedy, Robert Kennedy, Martin Luther King assassinations
  - Vietnam War
  - Woodstock
  - The Cold War
  - Roe vs. Wade

- Think of:
  - The Beatles
  - Bill Gates
  - Bill Clinton
  - Oprah Winfrey
  - Muhammad Ali

They're much less formal. Because there are so many, boomers have faced fierce, lifelong competition. They are entrepreneurial, yearn to distinguish themselves as individuals.

Today the boomers are in control. They run our local, state, and national governments, they are the bosses, supervisors, managers, and CEOs of most companies, and they dominate the workforce because of their enormous numbers. They are an amazing workforce because of their dedication to a solid, strong work ethic that is uniquely defined by them as working long and hard and being seen doing it. The word "*workaholic*" was coined to describe the boomers. They believe in "face time" with their bosses. They must be seen working hard or else that work ethic wasn't benefiting them.

The Matures laid the groundwork for the United States to become an influential member of the world community. The boomers came behind them and set the wheels in motion. Through their enormous numbers (76 million), their intense work ethic, and their competitive nature, the boomers got productivity in the United States to the forefront of the world community. The boomers also believe in the sanctity and the importance of the individual. Developing themselves into a more "whole" person is very important. Part of becoming a better person is learning to operate as a fluid member of a team, and the boomers are champions of teamwork.

Boomers today are still working as hard as they've ever worked but some are asking themselves if their intense work ethic has paid off the way they had hoped. The boomers entered the workplace when company loyalty was still standard. They've seen that change dramatically, though, as tough economic conditions have required layoffs and downsizings. Their work ethic may have gone unrewarded and they are wondering if they've missed critical parts of their lives while giving the company 110%. The boomers are evolving today and in the second halves of their lives they will live with a different focus.

The Xers:

- Born between: 1965 – 1978

- When you think of this generation think: Skeptical, Reluctant

- Cost of living index: A 1982 dollar would buy $1.90 worth of goods today.

- Popular toys: Rubik's Cube, Cabbage Patch Dolls, hand-held video games, early TV video games, new Barbie, theme toys based on TV characters.

- Formative events:
    - Watergate
    - Fall of the Berlin Wall
    - Challenger explosion
    - The Gulf War
    - The PC boom
    - The Reagan Presidency

- Think of:
    - Monica Lewinsky
    - Michael Dell

They're entrepreneurial, prefer to work independently, and they're looking for employers to help improve their skill sets. They don't always play well with others.

They came onto the scene and were given an unflattering, vague name. They were defined as "slackers" and were characterized as unmotivated, lethargic, sarcastic, and irreverent. They were the first generation that parents could take pills not to have. And as youth they were told they'd be the first generation in the nation's history that would not be as successful as their parents. Every institution in the United States that has said "you can trust us" (government, the church, military, marriage, major corporations) has fallen flat on its face. Whereas to the boomers and

Matures these institutions still mean a great deal and they just briefly faltered, to Xers they have never been deserving of anything but skepticism.

Though they could easily be considered pessimistic about their world and their future, you'll find that their attitude has a "carpe diem" feel to it. "There is nothing we can count on in the future," they say, "*so we'll focus short term and make sure each day has significance.*" It is not an attitude of irresponsibility. It is the contrary. In fact, Xers have willingly shouldered the responsibility for their day-to-day well being. "*We've seen that the company won't provide it, nor will the government,*" they think, "*So it is up to me.*" And this attitude permeates the workplace where Xers are steadily rejecting the Boomer work ethic attitude. Ironically, along the way, they're gaining Boomer converts.

Today you'll find the eldest Xers achieving management positions and the youngest have been in the workplace for at least three years or more. They'll inherit the many management positions vacated by the boomers upon their retirement, and they'll run things a bit differently. Don't fear. They'll be effective, profitable, and responsible, but different.

The Millennials:

- Born between: 1979 – 1988

- When you think of this generation think: Coddled

- Cost of living index: A 1995 dollar would buy $1.58 worth of goods today.

- Popular Toys: A variety of TV game systems, all video and computer games, skateboards, in-line skates, Barbie and other dolls, toys that make little girls seem grown up, toys based on themes from TV and movies.

- Formative events:
  - Oklahoma City bombing attack
  - 9/11 Terrorist Attack
  - The Internet boom

- Think of:
  - Tara Lipinski
  - LeAnn Rimes

The most adult-supervised generation has grown up trusting older people. Millennials love team play and are optimistic about their generation. We've just finished raising the oldest of them, but can only guess what kind of workers they'll be.

Born in a time where cell phones, laptops, remote controls, and travels to outer space are the norm, the Millennials are living in a world ubiquitous with technology. And the studies show they'll still see more change in their lifetime than any other generation. Along with ever-present technology, the Millennials have mostly known affluence in their lives. For the majority of their lives they've only seen a growing economy. The recent economic downturns are the first change in the nation's economic pace they've experienced.

Children of the boomers and the oldest Xers, the Millennials have lived protected by their parents. Threats to them are of a different variety than any of the other generations have lived with as children – rogue individuals with nuclear weapons, unchecked violence from their peers, and terrorism in their home nation (and, in one case, by their own countrymen). The parents' response is to insulate and protect their children, to carefully guide them through life, and to constantly build their self-esteem. Their lives thus far are epitomized by the yellow placards ubiquitous a decade ago on every minivan and station wagon on the nation's roads – "baby On Board." "Be mindful of my precious cargo," they essentially say.

Today the Millennials are entering the workforce in droves. A population whose size will rival the boomers, the Millennials come into the workplace looking for the opportunity to learn and move about. They want to be close with their peers and search for leadership from their bosses and supervisors. They're an army waiting to be guides, but they play by different rules.

Defining Moments:

Below is a look back at key events and influential forces of the past fifty years as defined by Mr. Gillon:

1950s

Movies: *Love is a Many Spendored Thing; Gigi; Ben-Hur*

Politics: Fidel Castro takes control of Cuba

TV: *I Love Lucy; The Ed Sullivan Show; Honeymooners: Twenty-One*

News: Polio vaccine and birth control pill introduced

Movement: Civil Rights

1960s

Movies: *The Sound of Music; The Graduate; Goldfinger; Midnight Cowboy*

Politics: Vietnam War; Civil Rights

TV: *Star Trek; Beverly Hillbillies; I Spy; I Dream of Jeannie*

News: President Kennedy assassinated; man walks on the moon

Movement: Anti-war protests

1970s

Movies: *Star Wars; The Godfather; Love Story; Jaws; American Graffiti*

Politics: Nixon resigns as President

TV: *All in the Family; M*A*S*H; The Waltons; 60 Minutes; Happy Days*

News: Watergate; Saigon falls; 3-Mile Island accident

Movement: Equal Rights Amendment

1980s

Movies: *Indiana Jones* trilogy; *Back to the Future*; *E.T.*

Politics: Iran-contra affair; end of Communism in Eastern Europe

TV: *The Cosby Show; Roseanne; Dallas; Cheers; LA Law; Miami Vice*

News: Challenger space shuttle disaster; stock market crash

Movement: Political correctness

1990s

Movies: *Titanic; The Matrix; Home Alone; Jurassic Park; Pretty Woman*

Politics: Bill Clinton's impeachment

TV: *The Simpsons; Beverly Hills, 90210; Seinfield; Friends; The Real World; X-Files; Law & Order*

News: Bombing of federal building in Oklahoma City; Dow tops 11,000

Movement: The Internet

2000s

Movies: *Lord of the Rings* trilogy; *Erin Brokovich; Chicago; A Beautiful Mind*

Politics: The war on terror

TV: *CSI; Survivor; 24; Sex and the City; The Sopranos; American Idol; Will & Grace; The O.C.*

News: September 11 terrorist attacks; U.S. invasion of Afghanistan

Movement: Globalization

In their book *Rocking the Ages*, researchers J. Walker Smith and Ann Clurman characterized the three generations, Matures, boomers and Xers as follows:

Generational Identities			
	Matures	boomers	Xers
Defining Ideas	Duty	Individuality	Diversity
Celebrating	Victory	Youth	Savvy
Success because	Fought hard and won	Were born, therefore should be a winner	Have two jobs
Style	Team	Self-absorbed	Entrepreneur
Rewards because	You've earned it	You deserve it	You need it
Work is	An inevitable obligation	An exciting adventure	A difficult challenge
Leisure is	Reward for hard work	The point of life	Relief
Education is	A dream	A birthright	A way to get ahead
Future	Rainy day to work for	"Now" is more important	Uncertain but manageable
Managing money	Save	Spend	Hedge
"Program" means	Social program	Cult de-programmers	Software programs
Go watch	*The Best Years of Our Lives*	*The Big Chill*	*Reality Bites*
The "In" crowd	Rat Pack Nightclubs Hep Zoot suit Kansas City Jazz	"Leader of the Pack" Rock clubs Groovy Bell-bottoms San Francisco Rock 'n' roll	Brat Pack Rave clubs Edgy Flannel Seattle Alternative

Smith and Clurman did not include the Millenial generation as they are considered to be too young to categorize or to have established its' nature.

Do you remember when tie-dye was a fashion statement; coffeehouses were the place to be; or your first time surfing was on a keyboard, not on a surfboard? If you answered yes to one of these questions, chances are you couldn't to the other two. The differences between these generations are more than just defining words and differing ways of looking at things or the search for new solutions for problems. They are our gut-level differences in values that involve our beliefs, emotions and preferences. These differences are how we view the world. They can result in open conflicts between family members and at work.

Kathy and Rick Hicks, authors of *boomers, Xers and Other Strangers: Understanding the Generational Differences That Divide Us* say, "The values we develop in our youth are the foundation for what we believe as adults."

If you're having problems with a parent or child, or anyone from a different generation, the cause most likely stems from the core differences of your values. Problems can come from almost any topics where there are basic value differences; from financial decisions to fashion, from music to food, and from recreation to religion.

Will these differences affect business and how it's done in the future vs. how it has been done in the past? You bet it will. We can no longer take the attitude of, "if it worked 100 years ago, it will still work today." We must remember that boomers are rule breakers; that individuality over conformity is a pattern for this generation. We have always done it differently, for example:

- Boomers didn't just eat food, we transformed the snack, restaurant and grocery store industries.

- Boomers didn't just wear clothes, we transformed fashion.

- We didn't just buy cars, we transformed the automobile industry.

- We didn't just borrow money, we transformed the definition of debt.

- We didn't just go to the doctor, we revolutionized the healthcare industry.

So what does all this mean for the future of the aging boomer? Can our country afford to have millions of us living to 80 or 100? Who will pay for the long-term care needed by a lot of us? Are we prepared to re-engineer products and services to meet the demands and needs of the aging boomer? And can our political system restrain the demands that millions of elder boomers will place on the social and economic infrastructure?

All good questions, true. What are the answers?

Chapter 7

The Multigenerational Dilemma

You've just read the chapter title and are saying to yourself, "What in the world is she talking about now?" Good question. While multigenerational households are still relatively few in number in the United States, because we are living longer, that may not be true 20 or 30 years from now. So how do we define a multigenerational household?

To be considered multigenerational, a household has to contain more than two generations of a family. And households where grandparents, parents and children share living quarters are relatively rare today, according to an analysis of Census 2000 data by bureau researchers Tavia Simmons and Grace O'Neill. Four million households contained more than one generation in 2000, representing less than 4 percent of all household types.

According to Census 2000, it's far more common for a parent to move in with grandma or grandpa than the other way around: more than two-thirds of multigenerational households, or 2.6 million households, consist of a grandparent as the head of the household, with an adult child and a grandchild. Far less common is the traditional "sandwich generation" setup: an adult head of household who lives with child and parents.

Many of the country's 4 million multigenerational households include families living together out of financial necessity. As America grows more diverse, so too do the living arrangements of American families. Census 2000 has tallied household types that are relatively new in the nation's history – such as unmarried couples living together and single women living alone. For the first time, the Census Bureau is delivering data on multigenerational households.

Consider these points:

- The number of relationships between generations is increasing. Four- and five-generation families are common, exposing children to longer relationships with older generations than those experienced by their parents or grandparents.

- The number of relationships within generations is decreasing. Since families are having fewer children, sibling relationships – relationships within generations – are less numerous.

- More relationships in families are adult-oriented. Parents will know their children as grown adults two, three or four times longer than they will know them as children. Grandparents are seeing the graying of their grandchildren. More parent-child and grandparent-grandchild relationships exist between two adults.

- Adult children will spend more years in parent-care than their parents did in child-care. Women in the United States currently average more years in parent-care than in child-care. The level of care ranges from daily care maintenance of feeding and dressing to occasional monitoring and supervision.

- More grandchildren are taking care of their grandparents. Many children, from elementary school to college age, are secondary caregivers to their grandparents after school and on weekends. This creates different roles and expectations among grandchildren and grandparents than have been traditionally portrayed.

- More grandparents are taking care of their grandchildren. The 1990 U.S. Census reported that 3 million children have grandparents as their primary caregivers. This trend is across racial and socio-economic groups and has enormous social and legal ramifications.

- The "sandwich" generation is caught in the middle of dependent parents and dependent children. They have trouble deciding where their primary loyalties and priorities should be – to their parents, spouses or children. More families are wrestling with roles and responsibilities of adult children to their aging parents.

Now, how about some numbers:

5.7 million: Number of grandparents who live with any of their grandchildren under age 18. Most of these grandparents (4.5 million) maintain their own household.

2.4 million: Number of grandparents responsible for most of the basic needs (i.e., food, shelter, clothing) of one or more of the grandchildren they live with. These grandparents represent 43 percent of all grandparents who live with their grandchildren. Of these caregivers, 1.5 million are grandmothers and 900,000, grandfathers.

900,000: Number of grandparents responsible for most of the basic needs of their grandchildren for at least five years.

1.4 million: Number of grandparents who are in the labor force and simultaneously responsible for most of the basic needs of their grandchildren.

NOTE: For more information on multigenerational families, go to: http://www.census.gov/Press-Release/www/2001/cb01cn182.html

After all the numbers, after all the statistics, you're asking, "So what? What does this have to do with me and my *life planning*?"

Consider the following:

Case 1:

> You and your spouse have a teenage son and live in a four bed-room, two bath home. Your widowed mother-in-law has taken a turn for the worse and is no longer able to live on her own. Family finances are not sufficient to put Mom in an assisted living home, so you move her in with you. All of a sudden, your 17 year old son is sharing a bathroom with an 89 year old woman who needs special equipment to access the shower and a riser on the toilet seat. Your son has a tendency to leave stuff all over the counter and wet tow-els on the floor. The resentment builds and no one is happy.

Case 2:

> You are recently widowed and have brought your elderly father into your home. This allows you to ensure he is being cared for and gives both of you the companionship you need. While things aren't always perfect, the arrangement seems to be working for both of you up to this point. Your 25 year old daughter leaves her husband and lacking any resources of her own, moves her 4 year old son and herself into your home. Dad exhibits little patience for the dis-ruption of his peaceful lifestyle and you're about to tear your hair out because of the noise, toys all over the floor and the added re-sponsibility for meals and babysitting.

Are you thinking neither of these will ever happen to you? Possi-bly, but then again, circumstances often alter the best laid plans. And if it does happen, how will you handle the change? Did you hold a family meeting before you moved Mom in? Did you set the ground rules for your daughter and her child before she took over your home? How can you ensure that Mom or Dad gets the privacy and quiet they deserve in their later years and at the same time consider the needs of the younger generation(s)?

None of the above sounds easy and believe me, it's not. However, with the right planning, a few modifications to your home and with open communication by all, it does not have to be daunting. Even if finances prohibit the cost of assisted living for Grandma, perhaps there's enough to add a small private bathroom for her. If Grandpa is given his own area of the house, he will have his privacy when he wants it, but will also be a welcome addition to the family unit when he wishes to join in.

The younger generations, and yes, that includes us boomers, can learn a lot from our elders if we only take the time to listen. They love to tell stories but do we ever take the time to hear them? Our elders have probably seen more changes in their lifetime than any generation before or that will follow. My mother grew up in a home with no electricity, no running water or indoor plumbing and four girls to a bedroom. Throughout her 89 years she has seen the advent of talking movies, radio, television, VCRs and DVDs. She remembers the first airplane arriving in her small hometown in Kansas, she has flown in a 747 to Europe, and has seen a man walk on the moon. She has gone from ice houses for refrigeration and wood cook stoves to ice cubes and running water in the freezer door and microwaves. From no phone, to the old crank style party line with an operator to today's cell phones that are smaller than a pack of cigarettes. Medical advances that are common place today were viewed as science fiction when she was a kid.

How many of us, our children, and our grandchildren truly appreciate what this generation has seen, heard, experienced, and lived through? Perhaps the idea of a multi-generational household isn't so bad after all. If we don't take the time to listen now, a vast amount of history is going to be lost.

If you are currently in, or are considering, a multigenerational household, why not set aside one evening a week to write down those stories? Make it a family project, write a book, create a movie, and treasure it always. If approached with the right attitude, the temporary inconveniences of a multigenerational will be far outweighed by the permanent memories.

Below are some things to consider before moving Mom and/or Dad into your home. This list is by no means comprehensive. It's just a few ideas that have come up in my consultations over the past few years. By the time you are done with your list, it may be many times longer than this one, but this is a good place to start.

- Do my parents and my children/my spouse/I get along?

- Is there anyone in the family unit who needs to be "in control?" If so, how will that affect everyone else?

- Will Mom and/or Dad have a portion of the house that is their sacred space, a place that is private, quiet and contains their prized possessions?

- Do Mom and/or Dad understand that while you are their daughter/son and they are your parent, you are no longer their "child?" This must be expressed aloud and over and over until everyone "gets it."

- What financial arrangements will be made? Will Mom and/or Dad help out with the expenses or are they financially dependent on you?

- What will you do to make them feel like a welcome part of the family unit and not a burden?

- Make a list of things that Mom and/or Dad can do as their contribution to the running of the household. It may be as little as dusting the living room, or emptying the trash, but they need to feel like they are necessary and needed.

- Do Mom and/or Dad understand that things are no longer like the "good old days,?" and that their portion of household expenses may be more than what they paid for their house payment 50 years ago?

- Do the kids understand that Mom and/or Dad will be making a contribution and therefore will have a right to a say in the household?

- Do you realize and accept that at times, Mom and/or Dad will slip and treat you like you are 5 years old again? Do your kids understand this as well?

A multigenerational home can be a challenge, but it can also be rewarding to those who experience it. It all depends on how you approach it and to what extent you formulate your plan for success.

Life After 50: When Old and Young Talk, Both Benefit
by Ovetta Sampson

Michael Atwell and Bill Brockelman are best buds. The next door neighbors do everything together. They fish. They fix up old rods and reels. They tell stories. They cruise the flea markets. And after Atwell gets out of school, he usually makes a beeline to his Colorado home just to hang out with Brockelman. The two have been friends for four years. They view their friendship as ordinary. But many people might see it as unusual, because Atwell is 12 and Brockelman is 71. "It's pretty different, for as old as Bill is and as young as Michael is," Michael's mom, Debbie Atwell, says of the friendship. "But I think it's pretty neat."

Academicians and analysts say such intergenerational friendships are not only "neat," they're desperately needed for the good of society. By fostering more relationships like Michael and Bill's, kids can find mentors and get the one-on-one attention they often lack at home, experts say. Elderly people can find more meaning in their lives and become more connected to their communities. And society itself could benefit from a more unified consciousness.

"[Intergenerational programs] can really foster a sense of interdependence in communities, and we need people to feel some sort of responsibility for each other," says Nancy Henkin, executive director of the Center for Intergenerational Learning at Temple University in Philadelphia.

Gap Growing Wider

Although there has long been a generation gap, demographics and pop culture have nearly obliterated the opportunities for generations to mingle.

Tom McBride, an English professor at Beloit College in Wisconsin, points the finger at pop culture. It's not that adults and younger adults can't get along, he says. It's more that society doesn't encourage them to interact. Advertisers split the buying market by age, drawing an imaginary line between 18- to 24-year-olds and those 50 and older. Television shows also segment the generations:

Teens watch the WB's "Buffy the Vampire Slayer," while their parents catch CBS' "Touched by an Angel."

Such practices have segmented our society in ways never seen before, says McBride. "Instead of one gap, there are lots of little gaps," says McBride. "People who communicate culture today are so much more skilled at targeting different segments of the society."

Job demands and increased mobility also have segmented families and generations. Brockelman lives near Colorado Springs, CO, but most of his sons, grandchildren and great-grandchildren live in Maryland. The generational schism has many consequences, experts say. For one, it tends to isolate many seniors from society.

"There are many older people who spend most of their life doing housework and watching TV," Henkin says. "They are mainly people who just aren't connected to the mainstream of society. They are people who struggle to say, 'How do I bring meaning to life?'" "Less contact between old and young also can hurt children," says Sally Newman, director of Generations Together, an international intergenerational studies program at the University of Pittsburgh.

Newman points to the increase in social problems, such as violence and drugs, that surround today's youth. She says seniors are an untapped resource of sustained mentoring. "There's a lot of evidence to say that communities that are in disarray may, in fact, be suffering from lack of communication within the communities among the generations," says Newman, who has been studying intergenerational programs for 25 years. "The more we let that happen, the more fractured...we're going to find ourselves." McBride also says that when generations don't interact, they can't communicate well or share ideas that could benefit society.

But all hope is not lost. In the past decade, nearly 300 intergenerational programs around the country have popped up to strengthen ties between young and old. A program in Virginia Beach, for instance, has third-graders helping senior citizens with computer training at a local nursing home. The benefits of such programs are huge, say those who studied them.

From Grumpy to Sweet

At Temple, Henkin takes a group of teens and seniors on a five-day retreat every year. The first thing that happens is that stereotypes melt away. That was the case for 150 eighth-graders at East Middle School in Colorado Springs who worked with seniors on a living history project. Before the project, the student described seniors as "mean and bossy."

But after interviewing the seniors, the youths say things differently. "I used to think they were real grumpy, but I actually learned they were sweet," says Monica Flores, 13. "They deserve respect. They've learned a lot more than any one of us."

During the project, the students were studying Anne Frank and World War II. They said talks with seniors, many of whom lived through the war, helped them better understand history. "You wish you could be there and see all that stuff," says Michael Davis, 14.

Ashley Pomales, 14, may have learned the most important lesson of all from the woman she interviewed. "She was like me," Pomales says.

Atwell and Brockelman say their friendship is mutually beneficial. Brockelman teaches Atwell how to fix rods and reels, and Brockelman doesn't spend his days in isolation, as many of his peers do. "I can't stay in the house," he said.

As for Atwell, a friend is a friend, period. This sixth-grader hangs out with his schoolmates and he hangs out with Brockelman. "It's not much different," Atwell says.

Building a Bridge

There are many ways to help bridge the gap between generations. Here are just a few:

- Try a regular family movie night. One generation picks the film one night; the other generation chooses another night. The groups review the movies, based on their perspective.

- Play "Generations Game," a cute board game much like "Candyland," except players must answers family history questions as well as general knowledge questions to win. You can get it online at www.generationsgame.com

- Call a nursing home or school in your area to volunteer.

Society Growing Older

So older people and younger people don't communicate. Is that a big deal? It is when you consider the changing demographics of society.

- In 20 years, 110 million people – nearly half the projected population of the United States – will be older than 50. Meanwhile, the birth rate is dropping.

- Now, those 50 and older control 70 percent of the wealth in the United States. They own 77 percent of all the financial assets, represent 66 percent of all stockholders and own 80 percent of all the money in savings and loans.

- Nearly 70 percent of Americans 65 and older voted in 1996, more than twice that of the percentage of 18- to 24-year-olds.

- Baby boomers are expected to live much longer than their parents. Their power and influence can affect public education, safety and health. Advocates of intergenerational relationships say the elderly are an untapped resource, and society could lose out if it doesn't learn how to use them to help it thrive.

Article Source: Baltimore Sun (Baltimore, MD), by Ovetta Sampson, Knight Ridder/Tribune, Publication Date: May 21, 2000
Statistics Source: Testimony given to the Senate Committee on Aging, Nov. 8, 1999.

The following was taken from an Internet Newsletter released by Charles Puchta, publisher of *Aging America Resources, Inc.*

Fifteen Things Every Family Needs to Know

The following is a list of 15 things every family needs to know as loved ones age, become ill or face injury.

1. GETTING INVOLVED. People don't know when to get involved in a loved one's life. Families often wait for a crisis before they recognize or acknowledge a loved one's limitations or needs.

2. THE BIG PICTURE. People don't realize that they should look at the big picture. They tend to focus on the issue at hand, not recognizing how their decisions are likely to have implications or consequences.

3. PROGNOSIS vs. DIAGNOSIS. People don't know to give as much or more consideration to the prognosis as they do the diagnosis. So many folks focus on the illness or condition without realizing how a condition is going to impact a loved one's life.

4. TREATMENT CONSIDERATIONS. Family and friends often treat the person differently once a person's condition or limitations are brought to light. This tends to frustrate care recipients as opposed to help a situation.

5. CAREGIVER BURN OUT. Caregivers don't realize that if they are not careful that they can quickly reach burn out. There are warning signs that caregivers should be aware of.

6. SENIOR MOMENTS. People don't know how to determine if a person is having a "senior moment," or if it is something more. Dementia, Depression and Delirium are often confused.

7. REACHING AGREEMENT. Families often make futile attempts to reach decisions without knowing what it is they are trying to accomplish.

8. DRIVING. People often don't know how to address concerns about a person's driving.

9. LIVING ARRANGEMENT. People needing care or assistance are often not aware of the many living environments and care options that are available to them.

10. WHERE TO TURN. People needing help, regardless of the issue, often do not know where to turn – let alone what to ask for.

11. LEGAL DIRECTIVES. People that complete their legal documents and advance directives often make the mistake of not sharing or communicating their intentions with loved ones who might be called upon to provide care or make decisions.

12. GOVERNMENT SERVICES. People qualifying for services are often unaware of the specific time frames and options that are available to them. Likewise many people do not realize the benefits and coverage that are, or are not, available.

13. SPENDING. People tend to focus more on saving for retirement without giving consideration to spending.

14. FACING DEATH. People often view death as a taboo subject and as a result do not give it much consideration.

15. EMOTIONS. Caregivers and care recipients alike often do not realize the emotional challenges they are likely to face.

Remember When?
by Karen Iuculano

I remember flying high conquering the day
My comrades right behind me, following all the way.
I never had to worry about my body giving out,
I was fearless, a leader; there was never any doubt.
Today as I sit here reminiscing about my past
I wish my body could keep up with a mind that's oh so fast.
Technology running rampant, some would say I'm just old
Nothing is as treasured as a mind still full of gold.
Please don't pass me by because I'm not the latest model
Take a chance, I'm waiting, my mind still runs full throttle.

Source: Reprinted with permission of Karen Iuculano, Publisher of *Sun Cities Profile*, 2005 edition. www.suncitiesprofile.com

Chapter 8

You're Never Too Old

How old would you be if you didn't know how old you was? (sic)
-Satchel Paige

When I began this book, it was my intent to provide a roadmap that would help you plan your next chapter in life; to provide the means by which to organize your "paper life" that so often gets in the way of how we want to live. The further along I progressed in the creation of the roadmap, the more it became apparent that I was really talking to my fellow baby boomers. There are mountains of research documents, statistics, magazine and newspaper articles that are apropos to this particular generation – far too many to mention within the confines of this book. However, I kept running across the same message over and over:

baby boomers have changed every stage of life we've touched. If we want something and it isn't available, we invent it and making something easily or readily available seems to be the key. We are a generation who desires instant gratification; to us patience is not a virtue.

So where does that take us on our destination? I believe we have already begun reinventing the idea of retirement, of aging, and most especially the concept of "getting older." On the cover of his book, Age Wave[1] Ken Dychwald has a bright banner that says, "If you expect to live to the year 2000, you need to read this book!" While we are several years past 2000, I believe he is still on target.

In Chapter 1, I talked about a trip I recently took with my mother and the physical and emotional toll it had on her. Today, 80 percent of

---

[1] Dychtwald, Ken and Flower, Joe. *Age Wage: How the Most Important Trend of Our Time Will Change Your Future*, Bantam Books, February 1990

the luxury travel in America is purchased by people over 55. For them, convenience and access – not cost – may be the main issue. Because we baby boomers are still young enough to demand changes in those very areas of convenience access, we will enjoy many more years of freedom than our parents ever did or will.

Though I look old, yet I am strong and lusty, for in my youth I never did apply hot and rebellious liquors in my blood, nor did not wit unbashful forehead woo the means of weakness and debility. Therefore my age is as a lusty winter, frosty, but kindly.
- William Shakespeare, from *As You Like It*

While we may be turned off by the idea of shuffleboard and bingo being the source of entertainment in communities such as Leisure World, Sun City and others, I challenge you to envision where you will live and what you see yourself doing for activities and recreation. First of all, we will most likely want and need a safe, controlled environment. Low crime, perhaps gated communities, perhaps not, but at least patrolled and kept safe and clean. Secondly, we will look for peers for friendships and with those friendships go the need for activities to share with them.

And finally, we will need a supportive atmosphere. What do I mean by that? We will need low maintenance housing, nearby urgent care and medical facilities, quick response emergency services, and convenient shopping and recreational options. We won't, after all, want to have to endure rush hour just to get to the local coffee shop.

If you or your spouse should require continuous care in a controlled environment, do you want to be close enough to visit every day? Maybe you would prefer to have a live-in caregiver in your home. If so, is your home designed in a way to accommodate a third person as well as a mobility-challenged or bed-ridden resident?

How do I envision the Next Chapter of my life? Where do I want to live, what do I want to do, and who do I want to do it with? Will I volunteer, continue to work but on a decreased schedule, learn a new career? Do I want two homes in different climates; or maybe I want to live outside the U.S.?_____

_____

_____

_____

If your desire is to travel as much as possible, low maintenance should be a high priority on your choice of residence. Perhaps a condo/townhouse would be more suited to your lifestyle than a single family dwelling.

Want to travel? Some cruise lines are considering setting aside some of their space as designated assisted living areas. One more reason to review your long-term care insurance policy. If it was purchased as recently as five years ago, it may be obsolete today.

As Mr. Dychwald pointed out in *Age Wave* (refer to previous footnote), the dissolution of the traditional linear *life plan* is slowly dissipating. We are witnessing, instead, a much more flexible arrangement known as the "cyclic life plan." We see more and more that longer life will eliminate the previous rigid correlations between age and the various activities and challenges of adult life.

Now is as good a time as any to address the issue of health care. We did touch upon it in Chapter 1 when I talked about extending life with new medical advances, but at what cost to that life?

> Did you hear the story of the 82 year old man who visits his doctor with the complaint that his left knee is painful and stiff? The doctor examines it and says, "Well, what do you expect? After all, it's an 82 year old knee." "Sure it is," says the patient. "But my right knee is also 82 and it's not bothering me a bit."

There's a lot of wisdom in that story. It's taken years and a lot of patience to finally find a physician that would 1) listen to what Mom and I are saying, 2) ask Mom what she wants/expects in health care, and 3) speak directly to Mom if I am in the room.

It should be mandatory that every young medical resident should be trained in how to treat and converse with an older person. Just because we may be wearing a hearing aid, have to put on glasses to read, and/or have slightly elevated blood pressure, doesn't mean we're incapable of understanding or making decisions about our health care. Just because I've chosen to take a friend with me to my consultation, doesn't mean I'm not in the room when a physician is speaking about my condition. Is it written in stone somewhere in medical school that Doctor is synonymous with God? I don't think so, yet I've met few physicians who don't bristle at being questioned about their recommendations and decisions.

Several years ago, Mom had an aneurysm in her right eye. Fortunately, we got to a specialist in time to save 90% of the sight in that eye. As a follow up, her ophthalmologist recommended that she see a thoracic specialist to test for other potential arterial blockages. Having an HMO as her Medicare supplemental insurance, we, of course, had to go through her primary care physician to arrange for this test.

The primary care physician also recommended she see a cardiologist for the same reason. We were so very fortunate in the choice of our thoracic specialist; he was truly one in a million – a physician who, first and foremost, had his patient's welfare at heart. He per-

formed an angiogram on Mom and pronounced her in good condition.

Then we visited the cardiologist who recommended she have
another very similar, yet less invasive test than the angiogram. I questioned the reasoning behind this test and was basically told to sit
down, shut up and listen to the expert. Not being one to take this
lightly, I called the thoracic specialist who advised me that this other
test was, in medical circles, known as the "Poor Man's Angiogram."
Needless to say, Mom did not undergo the second test.

And woe be to the person who tells a physician (s)he wants no
heroic measures, and is expecting the rest of his/her life to be one of
quality, not quantity. Which leads us to the next set of questions:

Do you have advanced medical directives? ❑ Yes ❑ No

Does your physician have a copy of your living will and advanced medical
directives? ❑ Yes ❑ No

If you and/or a family member has a serious medical condition that could
require heroic measures, and you choose not to exercise that right, do
you have a copy of your Do Not Resuscitate orders posted in a prominent
and very visible place in your home? ❑ Yes ❑ No

Does your physician have a copy? ❑ Yes ❑ No

Do you carry a copy with you? ❑ Yes ❑ No

During all this, I was having to drive Mom to these doctor's offices in the heat of a Phoenix summer and the wear and tear on her
was becoming obvious. Her comments to me ranged from, "I'm so
sick of doctors, I'd just rather be dead," to "I don't know what I'd do if
I didn't have you to run interference." Because she's of an era who
never questioned a doctor, a lawyer, or any other so-called "expert,"
she would have submitted to every test every doctor could think of
just to keep them happy.

On the other hand, I am very cognizant of the rising cost of health insurance and the reasons behind those increases. The unnecessary tests as discussed above are just a drop in the bucket compared to the $10 aspirin tablet or the $15 bandage your insurance is billed if you are in the hospital. And as we're now learning, hospitals aren't necessarily the best place to be if we are sick. Infections and viruses are running rampant and the over worked and stressed out physicians and support staff are missing vital pieces of information about individual patients.

Unless we take control of our health care decisions, the health insurance costs and the medical malpractice crisis will continue to grow. Until we are ready and willing to accept that we are ultimately responsible for our own well-being, we deserve everything we get, and that includes poor service from our medical community. Contrary to popular belief, they are not doing us a favor by seeing us at the time of our scheduled appointment; and they must earn our respect, rather than expect it.

The world is round, and the place which may seem like the end...may also be only the beginning.

- Ivy Baker Priest

How did I feel after my last annual physical? Did my physician talk with me about my condition, or did (s)he appear rushed and too busy to discuss my condition; doing not much more than hand me a prescription for some medication with no real explanation for its need?_____

_____

_____

What am I going to do in the future to ensure that I am in control of my health? Am I willing to voice my displeasure in my physician's attitude/demeanor toward me? Am I willing to request/insist upon an explanation for the necessity and/or side effects of any recommended medications or tests?_____

_____

_____

"Middle Age" Stretches Toward 80

The swelling tide of octogenarians presents the challenge of a lifetime to science and to society. When Dorothy Stewart retired six years ago at age 77, she didn't think she had any reason to stop working—or living a rich life.

A veteran real estate agent, she volunteered nearly full-time at an agency that matches elderly people needing help to stay in their homes with students looking for lodging in the pricey college town of Ann Arbor, Michigan. A heart attack and stroke curtailed that adventure after three years. But Stewart remains active, mentally and physically. She profiles every newcomer in her retirement community newspaper, exercises five a days a week, travels to Europe and reads voraciously. Stewart, a student activist at the University of Chicago in the 1920s, still is brimming with ideas and optimism. "I've made lots of new friends in the last couple of years," she says.

American scientists are giving intense scrutiny to people like Dorothy Stewart, a highly functioning citizen of the 80-plus world, our fastest-growing age group. Key trends are reported by the American Psychological Association (APA).

"If most could do as well as the best-functioning, then we'd have no concerns," says National Institute on Aging director Richard Hodes. But valid concerns are spurring a wealth of research and discoveries about life after 80. "If we need any encouragement, all we have to do is look at the numbers."

Baby boomers are the first generation in American history whose average member will live into the 80s, experts say. An avalanche of boomer octogenarians is approaching. Now there are 9 million Americans 80 or older; in 2025, there will be 15 million; by 2050, 31 million, the Census Bureau estimates.

But will those elders feel truly old? One-third of Americans in their 70s said they considered themselves "middle-aged," as did 22% of those 80 or older, in a Harris Interactive survey this year for the National Council on Aging.

"It used to be 65 was the bottom of the ninth," says psychologist Ken Dychtwald of Age Wave, a think tank and business consulting firm in Emeryville,

California. Now nearly half of 65- to 69-year-olds consider themselves middle-aged, so perhaps they can feed themselves.

And just as 64 isn't as feared in this post-Beatles era, some popular beliefs about life after 80 are myths, scientists report.

Myth: OUR GRAYING RANKS MEAN AN EPIDEMIC OF GRUMPY OLD MEN AND WOMEN.

Fact: Only if they were grumpy at 30. Basic personality does not change after 30, long-term studies confirm.

Myth: MOST WILL LIVE IN DEPRESSING NURSING HOMES.

Fact: About four out of five Americans over age 80 live in the community, says Richard Suzman, the National Institute on Aging's behavioral and social research chief.

Myth: DISABILITY IS RISING AS OUR POPULATION AGES.

Fact: The disability rate is sharply declining in adults 65 and older, Suzman says. Since the 1980s, the largest gains in health function have been made by those over age 80.

Myth: MISERY IS BOUND TO MULTIPLY WHEN THE BABY-BOOMER CRUSH HITS.

Fact: The jury is out on that, Hodes says. "The challenges are largely in their numbers."

Much depends on progress in delaying or curing Alzheimer's and on whether medicine improves disability rates enough to outweigh the burden of a huge increase in elderly people.

Some signs suggest we're headed in the right direction. One of the strongest predictors of good health is higher education, and Americans' education levels are rising, Suzman says. Some medical staples that add able years to many lives—outpatient laser surgery for cataracts, angioplasty—were unheard of not long ago. On the eve of a genetic science revolution, it's hard to know what's ahead, Suzman says.

Growth of the home health care industry, and of housing plans that offer a range from total independence to nursing care, will promote longer, healthier lives, research suggests. People at home are less likely to decline over time than are those who start out in comparable shape but live in group homes, says Pennsylvania State University psychologist Steven Zarit.

"A sense of mastery is a key predictor of who goes downhill. Do people feel they have choices, some control over their lives? Or are they assigned roommates, activities?"

Staying at home is no panacea, though. Zarit's studies show that many older Americans at home report unmet needs for help.

"You can buy it if you have $25,000, $30,000, $40,000 a year to spend—and it will last as long as your money lasts," he says. "The real issue for the future is going to be long-term care and how we help people stay at home."

A major problem for elders living at home is that "so many have outlived their siblings and children," says Colleen Johnson of the University of California Medical School at San Francisco.

Her recent study of 272 people over 85 shows that those with kids fare best. Blacks enjoy "larger and more flexible kin networks, 'adopted' relatives from church or clubs" that help them more than whites are helped if they don't have kids.

Alzheimer's disease could affect nearly half of Americans over 85, although scientists don't agree on an exact figure. Rapid progress has been made in understanding the biology of Alzheimer's, and a number of potential preventives and therapies are being tested. Adults with a good education or a large, positive social network are less likely to get all kinds of dementia, studies show. Depression impairs memory, "and if you don't treat the depression, it can look like dementia. Mood is sometimes overlooked as a key contributing factor," says Michigan State University psychologist Norman Abeles. People over 80 are thought to have low depression rates, but some experts think they're under diagnosed. Depression in older adults may have different causes and may manifest itself differently than it does in younger people.

For example, one provocative study the APA has reported on is of 405 elderly couples followed for six years. Spouses who feel strain caring for ill partners cheer up after the mate dies. "If it's a sudden death, and they weren't caregivers, then there's an increase in depression," says University of Pittsburgh psychologist Richard Schulz.

Depressed people die sooner than the comparably ill who aren't depressed. So it's not surprising that researchers find that the long-lived tend to be resilient people not inclined to despair, even when they face dire challenges.

Else Wolff of Santa Monica, California, who will be 97 next month, is a good example. Born in Germany, she was orphaned at 14 and married early. Wolff had two young sons and no vocational skills when her husband, Fritz, was taken to a concentration camp in 1938. She decided to go to the USA on a work visa, leaving her kids with a sister-in-law but determined to bring her family over soon. She went from a prosperous life to sparse rooms and menial jobs in New York. Her boys were supposed to follow in a few weeks, but bureaucratic snafus delayed their arrival for eight endless months. "That was the hardest time of my life. I wrote them every day."

Wolff met a journalist in New York who helped gather affidavits to get Fritz Wolff freed from the camp, which was possible at that time. When he finally arrived in New York a few weeks after the boys, he had his front teeth knocked out, Wolff says. "We celebrated his 50th birthday on Aug. 15 in Central Park. I remember, I bought a can of pineapple with four slices, and we each had one. But we were so, so happy to be together as a family again. It was one of the best celebrations we ever had." Now she has outlived two husbands and, in the bittersweet harvest of old age, a son and a grandson as well. But she still finds life interesting. Wolff voluntarily gave up driving at age 95. She still has her own apartment and has a live-in helper who does drive.

She's out most days—attending lectures and book reviews, visiting friends and shopping. Friends of all ages complain that they can't find her in or are put off by repeated call-waiting interruptions. Worry is not high on her agenda. "I try to solve what I can right away. I go for it," says Wolff, a tiny woman with piercing brown eyes. "If I can't do anything, I let it go."

One of her favorite amusements is people-watching at the Santa Monica Pier, overlooking the Pacific Ocean. She and her helper feast on the colorful panorama of people from all over the world walking by.

A granddaughter, 43-year-old Los Angeles lawyer Joan Wolff, says: "It's amazing that anyone would live that long. But if anyone would, it's her. She relishes life. She doesn't want to miss a thing."

Source: USA Today, by Marilyn Elias , Publication Date: 5/21/2000, pp. 1D-2D

Chapter 9

Whose Life is It Anyway?

Life does not cease to be funny when people die any more than it ceases to be serious when people laugh.

- George Bernard Shaw

It is only appropriate that one of the final chapters of this book be about end of life and our preparations for it. Often it is at this stage of our journey that family members become territorial, overbearing, and downright irritating.

Why do we spend so much time planning for a birth, graduation, marriage and even our vacations, and so very little time preparing for our final journey? Granted, no one is comfortable with this subject because that means we're admitting it's going to happen. But since we are all going to die at some time, wouldn't it be easier for you and your loved ones to know that you had made as many decisions and preparations as possible in advance? Okay, so what do we need to do?

Let's take a look at just a few of the questions that may affect you or your family at some point:

- Who should make your health care decisions if you can't make them yourself? Would this person understand and honor your values and views? Can he or she make complex and logical decisions in stressful and emotional situations?

- If you had an irreversible brain injury, at what point would you reject CPR, a feeding tube and antibiotics?

- Do you have any religious, spiritual, or philosophical beliefs that would influence what medical treatments you would or would not want?

- If you could donate organs or tissue, would you choose to do so?

Throughout this book, we have focused on adulthood and the aging process. However, this topic is very important to each of us and no matter how uncomfortable it is, should be addressed by everyone over the age of 18.

Advance Directives

Advance Directives were created to help you and your loved ones with these very emotional decisions before a crisis occurs. Those directives are:

- Durable Power of Attorney for Your Financial Affairs
- Durable Health Care Power of Attorney
- Durable Mental Health Care Power of Attorney
- Living Will (end of life care)

There are no mistakes. The events we bring upon ourselves, no matter how unpleasant, are necessary in order to learn what we need to learn; whatever steps we take, they're necessary to reach the places we've chosen to go.
— Richard Bach, *The Bridge Across Forever*

When I meet with clients, I urge them to hold family meetings to discuss these issues. Not only do you need to consider what you want, your loved ones need to know as well. How can they carry out your wishes if they don't know what those wishes are? Although family members are most often the designated ones to speak on our be-half, please keep in mind that a family member may not always be the best decision maker for you. It could be that they may be too emotionally involved, or don't hold the same belief system you do. Give careful consideration to whom you designate as your guardian angel, and make sure they are willing to accept the assignment.

NOTE: Whomever you choose as your guardian angel today, may not necessarily be the same one you wanted two years ago or will want 5 years into the future. This, along with every other part of your *life plan*, will change as your journey progresses.

Family discussions can often get heated and unpleasant. Conflicting views and beliefs may hamper productive results. Should the family meeting get bogged down, consider taking a break with one of the following comments:

- It looks like this isn't a good time to talk about this. Why don't we go on to the next item?

- It's obvious that you care about each other too much to let this subject pass, but we can drop it for now. At some point, you will need to make your wishes known to each other so you get what you want.

- Perhaps we need to set aside this matter for now and come back to it when we are less emotional and our heads have cleared.

There may come a time when family members absolutely will not agree to a particular point. This is the time you must make very difficult decisions. Do I want (whatever it is) bad enough to go against my family's wishes? If so, I must appoint an outsider to hold my Power of Attorney.

Advance Thinking on Health Care

In order to allow professional health care people to honor your wishes, it is important that you do some pre-planning. Please be advised that what you want is not necessarily what your spouse or other loved one would want for you. Therefore, a family meeting is imperative during the course of this planning. If there are major differences in philosophy and beliefs among the family, then perhaps a family member may not be the best choice to hold your medical power of attorney.

There are a number of tools designed to help you communicate your wishes about terminal illness and pending death. This planning, when put in writing, provides a means for you to participate in the decision making, even if you are physically unable to do so.

The following questions pinpoint health care issues that may be hard to discuss with your family. They will create discussion points and after thorough discussion, you should follow up your decisions with legal documentation. This will ensure that your decisions and wishes will be carried out.

Yes	No	
❏	❏	Do you think it is a good idea to sign a legal document that says what medical treatment you want or don't want when you are dying?
❏	❏	Do you think it is a good idea to sign a legal document that appoints someone to make health care decisions for you if you are unable to make or communicate those decisions yourself?
❏	❏	Do you want to donate parts of your body to someone else at the time of your death?
❏	❏	If you are terminally ill and your kidneys stop working, do you want to go on dialysis?

Yes	No	
❑	❑	If your heart stops beating, do you want to be resuscitated (use medical means to try to restart the heart)?
❑	❑	If your lungs can no longer function on their own, do you want to have a respirator (machine) breathe for you?
❑	❑	If you are terminally ill and are unable to eat, do you want artificial nutrition (tube feeding)?
❑	❑	If you are terminally ill and unable to drink fluids, do you want artificial hydration (I.V.s)?

Aging With Dignity, a non-profit organization based in Tallahassee, Florida has produced a document called *Five Wishes*. This booklet is meant to be used in addition to your will and advance directives. It does not replace your current powers of attorney, your living will or other advance directives you may have in place. Refer to the Resources section for information on how to order the *Five Wishes* document.

Five Wishes and other similar documents take the concept of the living will to the next level. It asks questions about your environment if you are unable to speak, i.e., do you want music playing and if so, what music? Do you want someone to read to you, and if so, what would you like to hear? These things may seem unimportant now, but put yourself in the shoes of someone unable to speak and imagine what you would like and what might irritate you the most.

Advance Directives: What You Need to Know

There are several tools available to you to communicate your end-of-life decisions. Each tool has a different emphasis and addresses a different audience.

1. Health Care (Medical) Power of Attorney

    a. Names a proxy or agent who is authorized to make future medical decisions on behalf of you ONLY if you are incapable of communicating your decisions.

    b. Gives the health care professional (physician) someone to consult when critical decisions need to be made.

    c. Remains in effect unless revoked orally or in writing.

    d. Is valid from state-to-state unless legal counsel tells you differently.

2. Living Will

    a. A simple, reasonable statement of the belief and desire of the dying person NOT to be kept alive by artificial and heroic means.

    b. Has NOTHING to do with money or property.

    c. Remains in effect unless revoked orally or in writing.

    d. Is valid from state-to-state unless legal counsel tells you differently.

3. Do Not Resuscitate (DNR or No Code)

    a. Goes beyond the desire expressed in the Living Will not to be kept alive by heroic measures.

b. Confined only to heart and lungs resuscitation.

c. Says that if a person's heart stops beating or if they stop breathing, he or she does not want medical treatment started or continued.

d. If person is unable to communicate, the Health Care (medical) Power of Attorney can consent to a DNR on behalf of the person.

e. DNR forms can be revoked either orally or in writing by so indicating to the doctor or nurse at the agency or facility.

4. Pre-Hospital Advance Directive

(Caution: Check that this is an accepted advance document in your state)

a. Form required for paramedics (911). It is the only tool they can honor.

b. Says the same thing as the DNR; if the heart stops beating or person stops breathing, no treatment needs to be started.

c. In my home state of Arizona, these forms MUST be printed on orange paper and can be obtained from most physicians' offices or from the Arizona Attorney General's web site. Please contact your personal physician for information regarding the correct form for your state of residence.

Checklist for Medical-Care Decisions

Medical Power of Attorney

Yes	No	
☐	☐	Do you have a medical power of attorney?
☐	☐	Is it signed, dated, and witnessed or notarized?
☐	☐	Is everything still as you wish it to be?
☐	☐	Do you wish to make changes?

Where is this document located?

_____

Who has copies?

_____

Note: If changes are required, be sure to have them initialed and witnessed or see your attorney about completing a new form.

Living Will

Yes	No	
☐	☐	Do you have a living will?
☐	☐	Is it signed, dated and witnessed or notarized?
☐	☐	Does it still reflect your wishes about medical care?
☐	☐	Do you wish to make changes?

Where is this document located?

_____

Who has copies?

_____

Note: If changes are required, be sure to have them initialed and witnessed or see your attorney about completing a new form.

Do Not Resuscitate (DNR)

Yes   No

❏   ❏   Do you have a signed DNR form?

You may need to re-sign this document at the hospital upon each admission.

Pre-Hospital Advance Directive (if valid in your state)

Yes   No

❏   ❏   Do you have pre-hospital directives?

❏   ❏   Has your physician discussed this document with you and signed it (as required in some states)?

❏   ❏   Is the form visible in the home for emergency medical personnel to easily see? In Arizona, the first place an EMT will look is the refrigerator door.

NOTE: In some states (including Arizona) a Mental Health Power of Attorney is required if you have mental or emotional problems. Talk with your attorney about how he handles this document. Some include it in the Medical Power of Attorney, others create a separate document.

What to Do with the Advance Directive Documents

❑ Keep the originals with your important documents and make note of their existence in your organizer (refer to Appendix D).

❑ Give each physician a copy for his or her records.

❑ Take copies to the hospital each time you are hospitalized. If a crisis occurs that requires an immediate decision, they may not be able to quickly obtain their copies from medical records.

❑ Give copies to other family members so they are aware of your wishes.

❑ If you have a Living Will or a Medical Power of Attorney from another state, check with an attorney to verify it is good in your current state of residence.

❑ Display the Pre-Hospital Advance Directive (orange card) in the home where it is visible. In a crisis, you or your representative may not remember where you put it.

❑ Make extra copies for other agencies (home health or hospice) that you may come in contact with in the future. They will need to know your wishes and have that information in their records.

Funeral Planning

One of the most difficult tasks in *life planning* is the planning of one's own funeral. However, even if we believe, "if we don't talk about it, it won't happen," it will. A wise man once told me, "Death is as inevitable as taxes." That wise man was my father and he passed away 10 days short of his 54th birthday.

When he moved his family out of Kansas into Denver, Colorado he purchased four adjoining cemetery plots, for my mother, my sister, myself and himself. While this was a great first step, and he was to be commended for that forward thinking in the 1960s, it was not nearly enough. Because joint bank accounts are sealed upon the death of one account owner, we had no money. I mean NO money. We had to borrow money from my aunt not only to bury my father, but to buy groceries. Granted, it didn't last long, just long enough for a representative from the state tax office to go through our family's safety deposit box and to interview my mother. But Dad had been in the ground for nearly a week before that interview occurred.

After this experience, my mother purchased a complete funeral plan. She wanted the exact same casket and services as we had for my father. At that time, it cost her around $1,600.00. Today, that same plan is selling for in excess of $20,000 and climbing. When Mom's time comes, the only out of pocket expense will be the transport of her remains from Phoenix to Denver.

I hope this personal story will be the incentive for you to start your planning now. You're never too young to have tragedy strike, and I would hope you would want to spare your family the necessity of second guessing your wishes. This is, after all, your last opportunity to get what you want and how you want it. But if you don't prepare the plan, what you will probably end up getting is what someone else wants for you.

The most frequent mistakes and/or assumptions made by all of us are:

1. I have an insurance policy that will take care of everything. I'm all set.

2. I bought my plot years ago, so I have everything.

3. I'm just going to have my ashes scattered.

However, this is what I've found to be true:

1. It can take up to three weeks to obtain a death certificate. After you have submitted the certificate to the agent or insurance company, it can take another week or so to receive the check. What happens to your remains while your family is waiting for this money?

2. A cemetery plot is just the beginning. Just a few of the other final expenses involved are: opening and closing of the burial plot; placement of the vault that contains the casket; transport of the casket; preparation of the remains for the service; and much more.

3. Some states have strict laws regulating the scattering of ashes. Because ashes aren't just ashes – there have been some instances of people finding bone fragments along river beds. You need to mentally prepare yourself for there being more than just ashes in the urn.

Other Important Things to Consider:

- Do you know that without a death certificate, you cannot collect on a life insurance policy?

- Do you know that a mortuary, cemetery and/or crematory require full payment at time of service?

If we face now the reality, at 65 or 70, 75, 80, 90, that we will indeed, sooner or later, die, then the only big question is how are we going to live the years we have left, however many or few they may be? What adventures can we now set out on to make sure we'll be alive when we die? Can age itself be such an adventure?

- Betty Friedan, author of *The Fountain of Age*

Plan Health Care for the End of Life

In 1998, Margaret Lazarz sat down with trusted relatives to orchestrate a critical stage in her life – her final medical care. With two surgeries and a pacemaker behind her and congestive heart failure a near certainty, the then-80-year-old knew there would come a time, not so far in the future, when she would need her loved ones to act on her behalf.

Margaret Lazarz needed an advance directive.

Advance directives spell out wishes for health care should a patient become too ill to speak. Doctors agree directives can make things clear, even in a complicated and emotional time.

"We all fall into a trap of continuing treatment if we don't know the patient's views," said Dr. Wayne Bottner, a hematologist at Gundersen Lutheran Hospital in La Crosse, Wisconsin.

Nearly 80 percent of Americans die in a hospital or nursing home and half are unable to make informed choices near the end of their lives. Fewer than 25 percent of Americans have written advance directives before they become ill.

Casual platitudes about future medical care – "Don't keep me alive if I am a vegetable," "Don't keep me alive on machines," or "No heroics" – are not enough. Legally, advance care planning has to be explicit to guide doctors and families.

Which is what Margaret Lazarz did.

She created a power of attorney for health care, designating her sister-in-law, Rosella Lazarz, and her niece, Janet Aide, as her representatives in making decisions. She didn't want doctors to attempt cardiopulmonary resuscitation, or CPR, if her breathing and heart stopped unless she had a good chance of survival. Her wishes were put in writing.

Margaret did two things right. First, she was specific in her instructions.

"Wishy-washy statements like, 'Do everything if I am going to pull through (but do less if it does not look so good)' are of little help," said Dr. Jack Udell, an internist at Gundersen Lutheran.

Second, she picked close relatives whom she trusted to advocate for her and to make difficult decisions under stressful situations.

"Picking a surrogate who is unable to make complex medical decisions" can complicate an already emotional time, Bottner said. They "often make decisions because of pressure from others rather than the patient's values."

This year, Margaret's relatives were put to the test.

Margaret moved from a hospital to a nursing home in Madison, Wisconsin, this spring after she was unable to breathe and her lungs filled with fluid. It was then that she changed her mind about her advance directive. When asked, "Do you want to be resuscitated?" she said, "Yes."

But, her niece later said, "I think she was scared and sick when she made this decision."

In the hospital, Margaret's doctor was met with a list of questions from the family: How bad was her heart? What could she expect for the future? If her breathing and heart stopped, would CPR be successful?

Gently, the doctor explained to Margaret that CPR would not help extend her life with any quality, if it worked at all. She then agreed to let her written directive stand.

In a few weeks her breathing and heart began to fail again. To make her more comfortable, she was transferred to a hospice facility, where she died the next day. Her advance directive, well understood by her family, had been respected.

Source: By Robert A. Bendiksen and Bernard J. Hammes, Knight Ridder Newspapers, Oct. 14, 2001

Things That Must Be Done After the Death of a Loved One

NOTE: Many of the following items assume the deceased had not purchased a complete funeral plan in advance. If a plan is in place,
those items marked with (*) may be included in the plan. It is a
good idea to review your funeral plan annually when you review
your other *life plan* documents and update it if desired.

NOTIFY:
1. Physician or coroner
2. Family attorney
3. Funeral director
4. Cemetery or memorial park
5. All the relatives
6. Employer
7. Friends
8. Organist and singer
9. Pallbearers
10. Church
11. Insurance agents
12. Unions, military, organizations and/or associations
13. Newspapers

Immediately following this list is a detailed guide for obtaining
documents and information to help settle a deceased person's estate,
courtesy of the AARP.

DO:
1. Meet with funeral director to review special instructions
   regarding final wishes
2. Plan service*
3. Order flowers
4. Provide clothing
5. Prepare cards of thanks

6. Provide vital statistics about the deceased*
7. Obtain at least 12 copies of death certificate
8. Prepare and sign necessary papers
9. Arrange for lodging for out of town mourners
10. Plan funeral car list*
11. Meet with attorney

The survivors must pay some, and perhaps all, of the following:
(* = assumes no prepaid funeral plan has been purchased)

- Doctor/nurse
- Hospital
- Drug prescriptions
- Funeral home/casket*
- Cremation*
- Cemetery lot/urn*
- Headstone*
- Interment service*
- Florist
- Organist*
- Clothing
- Transportation*
- Memorials
- Minister
- Printed funeral program*
- Police escort (if used)*

Final Details: A Guide for Survivors

Abridged version. For the complete pamphlet, check the AARP website and use the Publication Order Form

The death of a loved one is a very difficult time. Yet even during this period of grief and emotional readjustments, important financial arrangements must be made. This brief guide was developed to help you prepare for and handle some of the details. While this guide may help you, it is not comprehensive.

Collecting the Papers

- **The Death Certificate** will need to be given to many of the offices you contact. These can be purchased through your funeral director or County Health Department. While the offices may need to see a certified copy, sometimes it is possible to ask them to make a copy and return the certified copy to you. For most circumstances, you may want 10-12 copies.

- **Social Security Numbers** of the deceased, the spouse, and any dependent children. In some cases, you will need the numbers for anyone inheriting from the estate.

- **All insurance policies.**

- **Military discharge papers** if you are planning a burial in a veteran's cemetery or plan to file a Veteran's Administration claim. If you cannot locate these papers, they may be obtained by writing the Department of Defense's National Personnel Record Center, 9700 Page Blvd., St. Louis, MO 63132.

- **Marriage certificate** if the spouse will be applying for Social Security benefits or benefits accrued through the marriage or inherited due to marriage. These can be

obtained at the Office of the County Clerk where the
marriage license was issued.

- **Birth certificates for dependent children** can be
obtained at either the State or County Public Health offices
where the child was born.

- **The will.** If not found at home, check with the deceased's
lawyer or the safe deposit box. We strongly urge you never
keep wills or insurance policies in a safe deposit box,
however, when searching for a deceased loved one's
personal papers, their safe deposit box should be checked
as a last resort.

- **A complete list of all property,** including real estate,
stocks, bonds, savings accounts and personal property.
These may be stored in safe deposit box or other secure
place.

- **Copy of the most recent federal income tax return and
proof of last quarter's earnings.**

Insurance Policies

There are several types of insurance policies, including life insurance, mortgage insurance, accident insurance, auto insurance, credit
card insurance, and insurances through employers. Check the appli-
cability of all. File claims promptly. You may need to make a decision
on the type of payment plan you desire – lump sum or fixed payments.
Consider consulting an attorney or financial advisor about this decision.

Social Security

The deceased is considered to be covered by Social Security if
s/he paid in to Social Security for at least 40 quarters. Check with your

Social Security office or call them at (800) 772-1213 to determine if the deceased was eligible. If the deceased was already receiving benefits, check with Social Security before spending/cashing any checks received after death. There are two possible benefits from Social Security for survivors of the deceased:

1. A death benefit of $255 toward burial expenses paid to the surviving spouse or a child eligible for survivor benefits (usually a minor);

2. Survivors benefits for a spouse or children. In general, if there is any doubt about potential benefits, file an application for an official determination. Benefits are typically available to: spouses 60 or older; a disabled spouse 50 or older; a spouse of the deceased under 60 but who cares for dependent children under 16 or a disabled child; or children of the deceased who are under 18 or who are disabled.

Veteran's Benefits

If the deceased was a veteran who received a discharge other than dishonorable, the survivors may be eligible for benefits such as burial in a national cemetery, small payment toward a plot or burial expenses, and a headstone. The funeral director can help you apply. The surviving spouse and dependent children of veterans receiving disability benefits may be entitled to monthly payments. Check with the regional VA office.

Employee Benefits

Contact all current and former employers regarding any benefits for the survivors. These may include life, health or accident insurance. Ask if any final payment is due for vacation or sick leave or worker's compensation (if death was work related). Ask if the deceased belonged to any union or professional organization which might provide a benefit. Ask about pension rights

The Will

If the deceased had a will, locate it - perhaps through the family attorney, family or friends. It may be in a safe deposit box. If there is no will, this is referred to as dying "intestate". In this case, the estate will be distributed according to state law. Contact the Probate Court in your state or county. (NOTE: The estate does not include property where the title is in the name of the deceased and another person who has a right of survivorship. This type of property automatically passes to the co-owner.)

Probate

Probate is the legal process of paying the deceased's debts and distributing the estate to the rightful heirs. The spouse or executor of the estate files a petition with the court after the death. There is a filing fee for this process. Depending on the size and complexity of the estate you may require legal assistance. Proceeds from life insurance or IRAs which are paid directly to a beneficiary are not subject to probate.

Federal Estate Tax

Beginning in 1998, estate tax is only due on estates exceeding $625,000. (Scheduled to be raised to $650,000 in 1999.) A federal estate tax return must be filed and taxes paid within nine months of the date of death.

State Estate Tax

In general, any estate which pays a federal estate tax must also file a state estate tax, although state laws vary. For details, contact your state tax or revenue department.

Income Taxes

The federal and state income taxes of the deceased are due for the year of death. The spouse of the deceased may file jointly for the year of death. A spouse with dependent children may file jointly for two additional years. Contact IRS for more details.

Changing Ownership or Title

You may need to transfer ownership or change title of property, or revise documents after a death. Some items to check include:

- Insurance policies: Amount of coverage may need to be changed, as well as beneficiaries. Auto and home insurance may need revision. Under a federal law called COBRA, you and any dependent children may be entitled to continue health insurance through your spouse's employer for up to 36 months, providing you pay premiums.

- Check to see if medical insurance would be less expensive through your own employer.

- Auto: The title of the car may need to be changed.

- Will: Your will may now need to be updated.

- Bank accounts, stocks, bonds: Check with the bank representative to change the title and signature card on joint accounts. Accounts held in the name of the deceased only have to go through probate. To change stocks or bond titles, check with your stockbroker or the issuing company for their procedures.

- Safe deposit box: In most states, if the box was rented in only the name of the deceased, it will require a court order to open the box. Only the will or any other materials pertaining

to the death can be removed before the will has been pro-
bated. Check with an attorney for the laws in your state of
residence.

Credit Cards

Credit cards which were held exclusively in the name of the deceased should be cancelled. Payments due on these cards should be
paid by the estate. In the case of a spouse, you may have credit cards
in both names, or you may have used cards which listed only the deceased. In this situation, you will want to try to make payments in order
to keep your good credit rating. Notify the credit card companies that
your spouse is deceased and ask them to list the card in your name
only.

General Finances

Debts owned by the deceased will be the responsibility of the estate and should be forwarded to the executor who is settling the estate. However, debts which are jointly owed, particularly mortgage
payments, and utility or phone bills, should generally be paid by the
survivor in order to keep a good credit rating.

A word of caution to widows and widowers: it is generally sug-
gested that you do not immediately make permanent significant financial decisions, such as selling your home, moving or changing jobs.
You will need some time to consider your situation before you can
make these decisions responsibly. If at all possible, don't rush into a
decision you might later regret.

Professional Assistance

You may need or desire the services of a professional, particularly
a lawyer or financial advisor. Initially it may be easier to use the services of the lawyer who wrote the will, or you may wish to locate another professional with whom you feel comfortable. Seek advice from

family or friends who had successful dealings with the kind of advisors you are seeking. Professional organizations like the local Bar Association may be able to provide referrals.

Funerals and Burials

Check the AARP online publication Funerals and Burials written by the AARP Consumer Affairs section.

Support

There are many programs across the country which have been developed to provide support and assistance to the bereaved. If you are widowed, contact the closest **AARP Widowed Persons Service program**. Check the online list of **Bereavement Resources** for bereavement programs for other types of losses, as well as the online **AARP Publications Order Form.**

Chapter 10

Some Final Thoughts

When the idea of this book began to sprout and take on a life of its own, I realized that I was spending the majority of my time in my office and less and less time with my mother. Yes, this is my business and I must work toward its success, but at what cost? Like many of us have done with our children, I'd put her in front of the television in the evening, pop in a DVD and promptly disappear to get in just a few more hours of work.

What I didn't realize was that she'd come to depend upon our evenings together. She could be on her own during the day, but the nights got awfully lonely even if another warm body was somewhere in the house. Then I thought, "Is that the way I want to live the last part of my journey?" The answer was a resounding NO.

About this time I was struggling with all the balls I have to juggle as a single homeowner, a caregiver and a business owner. Then I received the following in an e-mail from a friend and it had a profound effect on me. George Carlin, the mouthy comedian of the 70's and 80's, wrote this after September 11, 2001 and after his wife had passed away. While you may or may not always agree with what George has to say, you must appreciate his thoughts as captured below.

A Message from George Carlin:

The paradox of our time in history is that we have taller buildings but shorter tempers, wider freeways, but narrower viewpoints. We spend more, but have less; we buy more, but enjoy less. We have bigger houses and smaller families; more conveniences, but less time. We have more degrees but less sense; more knowledge, but less judgment; more experts, yet more problems; more medicine, but less wellness.

We drink too much, smoke too much, spend too recklessly, laugh too little, drive too fast, get too angry, stay up too late, get up too tired, read too little, watch TV too much, and pray too seldom. We have multiplied our possessions, but reduced our values. We talk too much, love too seldom, and hate too often.

We've learned how to make a living, but not a life. We've added years to life not life to years. We've been all the way to the moon and back, but have trouble crossing the street to meet a new neighbor. We conquered outer space, but not inner space. We've done larger things, but not better things.

We've cleaned up the air, but polluted the soul. We've conquered the atom, but not our prejudice We write more, but learn less. We plan more, but accomplish less. We've learned to rush, but not to wait. We build more computers to hold more information, to produce more copies than ever, but we communicate less and less.

These are the times of fast foods and slow digestion, big men and small character, steep profits and shallow relationships. These are the days of two incomes, but more divorce; fancier houses, but broken homes. These are days of quick trips, disposable diapers, throwaway morality, one night stands, overweight bodies, and pills that do everything from cheer, to quiet, to kill. It is a time when there is much in the showroom window and nothing in the stockroom. A time when technology can bring this letter to you, and a time when you can choose either to share this insight, or to just hit delete.

Remember to spend some time with your loved ones, because they are not going to be around forever. Remember to say a kind word to someone who looks up to you in awe, because that little person soon will grow up and leave your side. Remember to give a warm hug to the one next to you, because that is the only treasure you can give with your heart and it doesn't cost a cent.

Remember to say, "I love you" to your partner and your loved ones, but most of all mean it. A kiss and an embrace will mend hurt when it comes from deep inside of you. Remember to hold hands and cherish the moment for someday that person will not be there again. Give time to love, give time to speak, and give time to share the precious thoughts in your mind.

And if that wasn't enough, George went on to offer this advice:

How to Stay Young

1. Throw out nonessential numbers. This includes age, weight and height. Let the doctor worry about them. That is why you pay him/her.

2. Keep only cheerful friends. The grouches pull you down.

3. Keep learning. Learn more about the computer, crafts, gardening, whatever. Never let the brain idle." An idle mind is the devil's workshop." And the devil's name is Alzheimer's.

4. Enjoy the simple things.

5. Laugh often, long and loud. Laugh until you gasp for breath.

6. The tears happen. Endure, grieve, and move on. The only person who is with us our entire life, is ourselves. Be ALIVE while you are alive.

7. Surround yourself with what you love, whether it's family, pets, keepsakes, music, plants, hobbies, whatever. Your home is your refuge.

8. Cherish your health: If it is good, preserve it. If it is unstable, improve it. If it is beyond what you can improve, get help.

9. Don't take guilt trips. Take a trip to the mall, to the next county, to a foreign country, but NOT to where the guilt is.

10. Tell the people you love that you love them, at every opportunity.

AND ALWAYS REMEMBER: Life is not measured by the number of breaths we take, but by the moments that take our breath away.

-George Carlin

And now, I'd like to leave you with another bit of humor. Just remember, life is not a destination, but a journey. A journey to be enjoyed, savored and lived to the fullest. Only you can decide how you want to live your life and with proper planning you'll be secure in knowing, as Paul Anka wrote,

I did it my way.

ARE YOU LONESOME TONIGHT?

(Senior Citizen Version)

Are you lonesome tonight?
Does your tummy feel tight?
Did you bring your Mylanta and Tums?

Does your memory stray,
To that bright sunny day,
When you had all your teeth and your gums?

Is your hairline receding?
Your eyes growing dim?
Hysterectomy for her,
And its prostate for him.

Does your back give you pain?
Do your knees predict rain?
Tell me dear, are you lonesome tonight?

Is your blood pressure up?
Good cholesterol down?
Are you eating your low fat cuisine?

All that oat bran and fruit,
Metamucil to boot.
Helps you run like
A well-oiled machine.

So your gallbladder's gone,
But your gout lingers on,
Tell me dear, are you lonesome tonight?

When you're hungry, he's not,
When you're cold, he is hot,
Then you start that old thermostat war.

When you turn out the light,
He goes left and you go right,
Then you get his great symphonic snore.

He was once so romantic,
So witty and smart;
How did he turn out to be such
A cranky old fart?

So don't take any bets,
It's as good as it gets,
Tell me dear, are you lonesome tonight?

Ladies and gentlemen,
Elvis has left the building.

Appendix A

The Insurance Planning Primer

Life Insurance

The need for life insurance is obvious: to ensure that you and your family are protected in the case of disability or death. But even while most people buy insurance to protect their homes, cars, jewelry, and other valuable possessions, some have no life insurance at all. Others don't have enough coverage under the policies they have purchased. It's important that you understand the different types of life insurance and how to determine the appropriate amount of coverage you need.

For example, let's say you work and your spouse stays home to take care of your children. As the breadwinner, you might determine your minimum level of coverage by thinking in terms of how much insurance it would take to replace your income. In addition, even though your spouse has no earnings, you might consider purchasing enough insurance to cover the child-care expenses you would incur in the event he passed away. Or, if you're a business owner, you may want to use insurance as part of a succession plan for your business. Of course, everyone's needs are different, and these examples just give you an idea of how to start thinking about your level of life insurance coverage.

Long-Term Care Insurance

On average, women outlive men by three to six years.[1] Therefore, women are more likely to require long-term care, such as home health aid or nursing home care. These types of care can be very expensive and are seldom covered by conventional health insurance.

[1] Money for Women, May/June 2000

Long-term care insurance may help you pay for these types of care in the event you need them down the road. In addition, paying for long-term health care through a long-term care insurance policy allows you to hold on to the rest of your assets, even if you are struck by an illness that requires extended care.

Generally, long-term care insurance makes the most sense for people with assets of $100,000 to $1 million who want to leave behind an inheritance for their loved ones rather than risk having those assets depleted to pay for long-term care. Most companies sell policies to people between the ages of 50 and 79, with costs being lower the younger you are.

> **Resource Tip:**
> A Shopper's Guide to Long-term Care Insurance, National Association of Insurance Commissioners,
> 1-816-783-8300
> or
> www.naic.org

Long-term care insurance is now being viewed as a necessity for almost everyone, no matter your age or financial status. I've seen baby boomers purchase long-term care insurance for their parents and/or in-laws as part of their own financial plan. Perhaps the parents cannot afford coverage, or just don't see its necessity. But if their kids are going to have to accept financial responsibility for their care, this may be one of the best decisions they can make.

Today, long-term care insurance products are not what your parents were offered 20 years ago and each policy should be reviewed along with your other financial documents.

Life Insurance Checklist

As you start to consider the types and amounts of life insurance that are appropriate for you, you'll need to answer the following questions:

❑ Would your family's financial security be at risk if you were to die? _____

_____

❑ How much money will your dependents need in order to live comfortably after you're gone?_____

_____

❑ What are your monthly expenses, including mortgage payments and utilities? Could your family afford to continue living in your home? _____

_____

❑ How much debt would you be leaving behind (including any medical or estate expenses) that your family will need to be able to pay off?_____

_____

❑ Could your children's college education(s) be paid for?

_____

❑ How about any emergency expenses, such as an expensive home repair?_____

_____

❏ How much coverage can you afford? How high a premium can you pay on a monthly basis? Quarterly?_____

_____

_____

❏ What is the claims-paying ability of the insurance company you're considering, and how is the company rated by industry experts?_____

_____

❏ Will your family need assets to handle taxes on your estate?

_____

_____

❏ Business owners: Will your successor have enough assets to purchase your interest in the business in the event of your death or disability?_____

_____

_____

Types of Life Insurance

Here is an overview of the three basic kinds of life insurance available and who would benefit most from each kind.

Whole Life Insurance

Whole life insurance is designed for permanent life insurance protection, i.e., when coverage is needed for your whole life. The traditional whole life policy calls for the same "level" annual premium every year. In effect, therefore, you are paying more than the term cost of your coverage in the early years and less in the later years, making the overall payments more affordable. If you surrender the policy

Consider this option if you
- Have a limited budget
- Want lower initial premiums, allowing you to buy higher levels of coverage at a younger age
- Have a specific temporary need you'd want covered in the event of your death, such as a car loan, college costs, or a mortgage
- Don't need to build cash value
- Have no other insurance needs once the temporary policy expires or have permanent insurance to cover your other needs

during your life, some of your premium payment (plus interest) will be returned to you in the form of a cash surrender value. This value builds over time, and you can access it (via policy loans) even if you do not surrender the policy. Traditional whole or permanent life insurance provides lifetime insurance protection with solid cash value accumulation, fixed premiums, and guaranteed death benefits.

If you are married, you might consider survivorship life insurance, also known as "second-to-die" insurance, as an alternative or supplement to single life insurance (when the policy insures the life of only one person). Since spouses can generally leave an unlimited amount of assets to each other without federal estate tax, most of that tax today is paid at the death of the second spouse. Survivorship policies insure both spouses under one policy, paying the death benefit at the second death when it is needed to pay taxes. The cost of this coverage is generally less than the cost of coverage on either spouse alone.

Term Insurance

Term insurance is usually the most affordable life insurance option available, particularly at younger ages. It allows the policyholder to protect his or her family for a specified amount of time. It provides temporary coverage and builds no cash value. There are different types of term policies. Some have a premium that increases annually, while others provide coverage for a specific period of time with a level premium. When your needs change, many term policies can be converted to permanent life insurance.

> **Consider this option if you**
> - Need insurance protection for a long period
> - Prefer your premiums to remain the same
> - Want a permanent policy that offers guarantees
> - Want to build tax-deferred cash value over time
> - Want to take out a loan on the cash value

Universal Life Insurance

Universal life insurance, a "flexible premium" life insurance policy, can help you meet a variety of needs. Like whole life insurance, it builds cash value, but unlike whole life, it allows you to vary the amount and/or timing of premium payments, as well as to adjust the death benefit amount to adapt to your changing needs. Your premium payments go into an account value fund, to which interest is credited and from which the cost of your insurance coverage and other charges are deducted.

Income Protection

By reviewing your entire situation with an investment professional, you'll be able to determine the best kinds and amounts of life insurance for your particular needs. A general rule of thumb is to purchase insurance in an amount that is six to eight times your annual earnings. However, you should also take into account the following:

❑   Other sources of income you might have,

❑   If you are married (and if so, what your husband's annual earnings are)

❑   How many dependents you have (including aging parents who might be financially dependent upon you),

❑   Any employer-sponsored policies you may have,

❑   Exactly what expenses you are trying to cover (e.g., college, mortgage, estate taxes).

As a starting point, this chart shows the monthly income that various amounts of insurance would provide to your family in the event of your death.

Source: Liberty Mutual Insurance Company

Income Protection (continued)

If you have this much life insurance	After taking out $25,000 for last expenses	Your family will have this much left to provide income	Which will provide this much monthly income for 10 years	Or this much monthly income for 20 years	Or this much monthly income for 30 years
$25,000	$25,000	$0	$0	$0	$0
$50,000	$25,000	$25,000	$263	$163	$132
$100,000	$25,000	$75,000	$788	$488	$396
$250,000	$25,000	$225,000	$2,365	$1,465	$1,188
$500,000	$25,000	$475,000	$4,992	$3,093	$2,508
$1,000,000	$25,000	$975,000	$10,247	$6,249	$5,147

Source: Liberty Mutual InsuranceCompany

Long-Term Care Insurance Worksheet

❑ Once you've decided to purchase long-term care insurance, you'll need to consider these questions when choosing a policy.

❑ How much does home health or nursing home care cost (to help you determine the level of benefits to buy)?

❑ How much will the insurance policy cover for various levels of care (home health aide, assisted living, nursing home)?

❑ How long will the policy's benefits last for various levels of care?

❑ How much does the policy cost? (To understand how paying for a policy will affect your budget, you will want to look at the costs over time, i.e., over one year, five years, and so on.)

❑ What is the deductible or elimination period (the number of days you must pay for care yourself before coverage kicks in)?

❑ What is the pre-existing condition limitation period?

❑ Can the company cancel or refuse to renew the policy? Under what circumstances?

❑ Does the policy provide benefits if you move to another state?

❑ Will the policy provide benefits if you have coverage with another policy?

Other Issues Related to Long-Term Care That You Might Need to Consider

❑   Do you have a durable power of attorney in place (in the event you cannot sign or make decisions for yourself)?

❑   Do you have a health care proxy (in the event health care decisions need to be made for you)?

❑   If available in your state, do you have a living will stating your wishes regarding life-prolonging measures?

Appendix B

The Estate Planning Primer

Most people are uncomfortable even thinking about, much less discussing and planning for, the transfer of assets to their heirs. That's why family members often are left with the daunting task of having to take care of their loved one's estate during an emotional time – and of possibly being forced to make decisions they are unprepared for. Therefore, it's important for you and your family to put estate planning measures into place, including letting each other know wishes regarding a funeral, disposition of possessions, and so on. Women should be particularly concerned with estate planning because 70% of married women will outlive their spouses.

Estate Planning Checklist

❑ Do you have an up-to-date will?

❑ Have you named guardians for your minor children?

❑ Have you chosen an executor and a trustee (individual(s) whom you trust to handle your estate according to your wishes)?

❑ Have you made arrangements to have any family member's special medical or education expenses taken care of?

❑ Do you have plans in place for long-term health care for you, your spouse, or any other family members who may require this kind of care?

❑ Have you outlined charities to which you wish to donate?

❑ If available in your state, do you have a living will stating your wishes regarding life-prolonging measures?

❑ Is there a plan in place for the disposition of any business you may own or have a partnership stake in?

❑ Have you reviewed with your financial planner the most tax-efficient ways to set up your accounts?

❑ Have your CPA and attorney talked with your financial planner to review your estate in its entirety?

Eight Excuses for NOT Doing an Estate Plan

1. **Excuse**: I've just been too busy, but as soon as I have more time, I will get something done.

Reply: Like most things, you have to make time to do matters that are important. Letting yourself be too busy is simply a convenient excuse to put off something you think you will always be able to do later. Unfortunately, car accidents, strokes and other unexpected tragic events in our lives do not let us put off indefinitely this type of planning.

2. **Excuse**: I don't really know what I would want to do for an estate plan.

Reply: You already have an "estate plan." Even if you don't know what you want to do for your estate planning, the state you live in has decided where your property goes if you do nothing. Anyone who dies without a will or other estate planning document is governed by state statutes. Those statutes direct who is to receive your property and when. If the statutes pick the wrong person, or the wrong assets that a person should receive, or the age at which they should receive those assets, then your desire and the state's plan will not be the same.

3. **Excuse**: It will cost too much.

Reply: Not doing anything can cost you even more. For example, you may be able to avoid or reduce estate taxes which can be as high as $.55 on the dollar. Basic tax planning can often save hundreds of thousands of dollars in estate taxes. Also, many times you can avoid probate administration fees and delays. Those fees are based on statutory schedules that can cause a $100,000 probate estate (in California) to be subject to $3,000 or more of attorney fees and $3,000 of executor fees. A $1,000,000 estate may be subject to $20,000 or more of attorney fees and another $20,000 of executor fees. The minimum time to probate an estate is usually six months.

4. **Excuse**: I don't like having to think about my death.

Reply: One of the primary reasons to do estate planning is to make sure that you have made appropriate provisions for your family in the event of your death. The focus is on planning to help protect their interests. Having completed your estate planning does not mean you are going to die any sooner than you would have otherwise, but it does give you the peace of mind to know that you have taken care of providing for your family's needs if you do.

5. **Excuse**: I'm not comfortable having to talk about my personal financial situation and family matters with a lawyer.

Reply: Your lawyer treats anything he learns about you as confidential, and acts only for your best interest. It makes as little sense to avoid seeing a lawyer to keep your financial situation private as it does to avoid seeing a doctor to keep your health situation private. Ultimately, that strategy is going to backfire.

6. **Excuse**: I don't own enough assets to make it important to do.

Reply: No matter how small an estate you may have, usually there are reasons why having a will or trust in place for the disposition of your property is better than having no will or trust at all. For example, if you have minor children, you need to think about nominating a guardian to take care of those children if there isn't a surviving parent. There are numerous other issues like these that should be addressed, even for someone with a small estate.

7. **Excuse**: My spouse and I do not agree on what we should do.

Reply: If you do not agree and do nothing because of that disagreement, then your spouse will be able to control everything if you die first. If you do a will or trust, you can at least make decisions to control your one-half of the property.

8. **Excuse**: I do not know who to name (or cannot decide who to name) as trustee, or executor, or guardian of my children.

Reply: If you do not name them, then state law will name them for you, by establishing a priority for who may act in those roles, and they may be just the people you want to avoid receiving those powers.

Appendix C

Fourteen Forecasts for an Aging Society

As the United States grows older, seniors who continue to work, take advantage of new technology, and plan ahead for long-term health care will fare the best. As the baby-boom generation ages and the pool of retirees increases exponentially, a period of great change in elder care looms. The median age of the U.S. population has been steadily rising. In 1900, one American in 25 was 65 or over. By 2050, that figure will increase to one in five. The U.S. Census Bureau projects that the over-65 population will more than double between 2000 and 2050. The proportion of "oldest-old" Americans, those 85 and over, will grow even more rapidly—quadrupling over the same period. By the year 2020, the ratio of over-65 individuals to the working age adult population will be about one to four.

As a result, we will see sweeping changes in health care, including Medicare, the government program that currently covers 39 million Americans. There will also be major growth in options for elder care, as well as a flood of new products and services aimed directly at this swelling segment of the population.

Here are 14 forecasts based on recent surveys and studies, many of them conducted by the SCAN Health Plan, a not-for-profit plan serving about 39,000 seniors in Southern California.

1. The Retired Will Work Again

    More seniors are likely to re-enter the labor force, thanks to new legislation allowing those 65 to 69 to earn without penalizing Social Security benefits. Currently, 23% of the 9.2 million people in this age bracket are in the labor force. That is over 2 million senior workers. Seniors' job-search success will no doubt be boosted by their increased comfort and proficiency with computers.

In addition to the financial benefits of earning a steady paycheck, seniors might get some health benefits, too. A SCAN Health Plan study among its members found that nonworking seniors are more likely to have significant health and daily living problems.

2. Tech-Savvy Seniors Will Maintain Their Independence

Elder-friendly technology will significantly improve access to resources and information to assist those who are frail and vulnerable. It will also reduce isolation among those living in rural or hard-to-reach areas of the country. Products such as the multi-functional pager, which alerts seniors when it is time to take a particular medication, will be readily available. The increased use of technology will be a key factor in helping tech-savvy seniors to remain living independently, as it will enhance their ability to communicate and obtain valuable health-care information. Technology will also allow health-care providers to better monitor their patients.

Currently, nearly a quarter of the 20 million seniors aged 60 to 69 own and use a computer, as do 14% of the 16 million seniors 70 to 79, according to AgeLight Institute. Computer ownership among members of SCAN Health Plan is even greater. A survey found that 36% of seniors 65 to 74 reported having a PC in the home. Of those 74 to 89, 34% owned a computer. While technology will play a wider role for seniors in the twenty-first century, the potential for isolation will increase the need for service fostering human interaction.

3. The Hottest Fitness Buffs? Seniors!

Health plans may begin to offer health club memberships and personal trainers as part of their coverage for seniors because of the proven benefit regular exercise has on seniors' overall health.

Health clubs report that seniors are the fastest-growing group of members.

A recent survey finds more than two-thirds of seniors engage in regular physical exercise, double the national average for younger adults.

A SCAN survey of 2,035 seniors aged 65 to 90 found that 68% maintain a regular regimen of exercise ranging from moderate activities like walking to more intense workouts including weight lifting, jogging, cycling, tennis, and even heart-pounding handball. Forty percent of the survey respondents said they spend more than four hours per week on these activities. Another 44% exercise one to four hours each week.

Among a group of seniors in a SCAN-sponsored mall-walking program, an insulin-dependent diabetic was able to reduce insulin intake by four units per day. Others reported improved heart conditions, lower blood pressure, less pain from arthritis, and the elimination of leg cramps.

4. Senior-Friendly Cars Will Offer Independence

Automakers may one day market cars that are easier and safer for America's growing population of seniors to drive. The "senior-mobiles" may include such features as higher seats, larger numbers on the speedometer, and slower acceleration. Retaining the ability to drive is the chief concern among aging seniors, according to SCAN research. For many, losing the ability to drive means losing one's independence and being forced to rely on others for transport.

5. Seniors Will Be Important Voters

Seniors will wield the most power of any demographic group in the voting booth. Seniors are big-time voters. In the 1996 federal elections, more than two-thirds of those 65 and older voted, according to the Census Bureau. That is 36% better than the 25 to

44 age group. Seniors not only rank as the top voters, but they are likely to be the most-informed voters. Contrary to the popular belief that seniors are not interested in current events, a SCAN Health Plan survey reveals that they are major consumers of the daily news.

According to the survey, four of the top five television programs most frequently watched by seniors are some type of news program. Only 29% of respondents said they watched daytime talk shows. Soap operas drew just 10% of the seniors. By comparison, 90% said they had watched the evening news.

Seniors are also avid readers. Eighty-seven percent of seniors ranked reading the newspaper among their most favored regular activities. Magazine reading was favored by 75%.

6. More Alternatives to Nursing Homes Will Emerge

One of the government's biggest tasks in the new millennium will be an extensive education campaign to increase awareness of the wide range of alternatives to nursing homes. Because of Medicaid's reliance on publicly funded nursing homes and hospital care, most seniors are not aware of alternatives, such as assisted living, independent living, life-care communities, and adult day care. A Harvard School of Public Health survey found that a majority of adults over 50 had never heard or read about six of 10 alternatives to nursing homes listed in the survey.

Nursing home care cost Medicaid $40.6 billion in 1998 (24% of total outlays), compared to $14.7 billion in 1985. Clearly, more cost-effective options are needed, although these alternatives must provide a high standard of care.

7. boomers Could End Up Impoverished

Many aging baby boomers who thought they would be spending their golden years in relative financial comfort may actually find themselves impoverished because they did not prepare for the costs of long-term care. A survey by the American Health Care

Association found that 68% of baby boomers are not financially prepared for long-term care should they need it later in life. Half of the boomers polled had not even given any thought to how they will pay for long-term care needs. Part of the problem may stem from a lack of understanding about how long-term care is paid for.

A separate survey by the National Council on Aging, in conjunction with John Hancock Mutual Life Insurance, found that one-third of baby boomers incorrectly assume that Medicare is the primary source for long-term care funding. The fact is, Medicare covers only about 53% of all health care costs. Most people are surprised to find that it does not cover long-term care, prescription drugs, or vision or dental care.

8. Elder Care Shortage is Coming

As the population of those 85 and older doubles to 8.4 million by 2030, the demand for professional home care aides will skyrocket. By 2008, personal care and home health aide jobs will rank second only to systems analysts in terms of sheer numbers (1.19 million vs. 1.18 million), according to the Bureau of Labor Statistics.

Twenty-nine percent of seniors age 65 and up rely on a daughter or daughter-in-law for caregiving assistance compared to 12% who rely on a son, according to a SCAN survey. However, daughters will become increasingly unable to take on the caregiver's role; more and more women will take on time-consuming managerial and executive positions as they continue to outpace men in earning bachelor's degrees (637,000 vs. 500,000 in 2000).

As the need for in-home elder care service providers soars, a major shortage of caregivers could result.

9. Aging boomers Will Force Health Care Policy Changes

Baby boomers can be expected to use their influence to ensure that quality health care services and programs are available for their parents now, not to mention for themselves in the not-too-distant future. There is power in numbers among the baby boomers. Approximately 76 million boomers born between 1946 and 1964 will soon join the ranks of older Americans. Many of these baby boomers are beginning to provide care for their aging parents. However, they also have a significant vested interest in ensuring that quality health care will be available for themselves. According to the Census Bureau, one in every nine boomers will live at least 90 years.

Perhaps the biggest concern among baby boomers is long-term care, which is currently not covered by Medicare. In fact, one survey found that long-term care has replaced child care as the number one concern among baby boomers. Nearly 66% of baby boomers polled in the 1999 survey by the National Council on the Aging and John Hancock Life Insurance said they would expand Medicare to cover long-term care, even if it means paying higher taxes.

10. Elder Care Will Hurt Women's Careers

Women's progress toward finally shattering the glass ceiling will be slowed because of the increasing burden of elder care. Despite women's advancement up the corporate ladder, a SCAN survey indicates that women are still disproportionately affected by elder care.

Strong evidence of elder care's adverse impact on career advancement comes from a national study conducted by the National Alliance for Caregiving and the American Association of Retired Persons. The study found that 31% of caregivers significantly alter their career paths; some leave the work force altogether. According to the study, which polled 1,200 people who provided caregiving assistance to someone 50 or older, 11% of caregivers took a leave of absence, 7% opted to work fewer hours, 4% lost job benefits, 3% turned down a promotion, and 10% took early retirement or quit their jobs.

11. Telecommuting Will Assist Family Caregivers

Increased telecommuting will allow working adults to move closer to their aging parents and thus ease the burden of long-distance caregiving. The National Council on the Aging (NCOA) estimates that nearly 7 million caregivers provide care for someone who lives at least one hour away. As more and more companies offer telecommuting, employees will be able to work from anywhere in the country and will have the flexibility to meet elder-caregiving responsibilities.

The percentage of companies with telecommuting rose steadily during the 1990s. In 1993, just 6% of the companies surveyed by William M. Mercer Inc. offered telecommuting. That figure grew to 14% by 1995 and 33% by 1998.

12. More Employers Will Offer Elder Care

Elder care benefits will become a major issue for workers and their employers as increased elder care-related absences and falling productivity begin to take a toll on the workplace.

The Census Bureau projects that over 40 million people in the United States will be older than 65 by the year 2010, an increase of 19% from 1995. As a result, about 12% of informal caregivers will quit their jobs to provide care full-time, estimates the Family Caregiver Alliance. In a tight labor market, employers will offer more elder care benefits to combat employee turnover. In order to attract and retain quality employees, as well as strengthen productivity, companies will develop ways to help their employees deal with the burden of caring for aging parents. This trend will mirror the movement among corporations to provide child-care assistance in the 1980s and early 1990s.

In 1999, 47% of companies offered some type of elder care, up from 40% in 1998, according to an annual survey of over 1,000 employers by benefits consultant Hewitt Associates of Lincolnshire, Illinois. By comparison, 90% of companies offered some type of child-care assistance.

13. Caregivers Will Need Interviewing Skills

The sandwich generation, those caught between raising children and taking care of aging parents, will have to learn a lesson from human-resource executives. As the senior population grows, there will be a constant stream of new business start-ups offering products and services to this group. Caregivers will be forced to make decisions on whom to hire and which organization or firm to use, much as human-resource professionals do on a daily basis.

Employers, working in concert with their human-resource departments, will set up training sessions for employees to allow them to make better decisions when it comes to hiring home aides or choosing elder care service providers. These sessions will stress that employees need to:

- Brush up on interviewing skills. Most of us have been through an interview process, but only as a candidate.

- Ask about availability of services. Twenty-four-hour, seven-day-a-week services are a must.

- Have potential caregivers submit resumes, complete with references.

- Ask, "Will the qualified care manager have a qualified back-up during vacations and time off?"

- View parents and relatives receiving care as "upper management," in that no decision on hiring should be made without upper management's input.

14. Working Families Will Gain State Allies

As the balance between work and family becomes an increasingly major issue, more state legislatures are likely to follow in the footsteps of the four that have already taken steps to ensure that companies accommodate employees' caregiving responsibilities. While the legislation covers family caregiving, it is especially valuable to workers caring for an aging parent. Terms of the legislation approved in California, Oregon, Washington, and Minnesota allow workers not covered by union contracts to use up to one-half of their paid sick leave to care for an ill child, spouse, or parent.

Elder care is likely to become an increasingly worrisome issue for employers as aging seniors eschew nursing homes in favor of independent living. Annual growth in nursing home residents has slowed to just 0.4%, down from 4.8% in the mid-1970s, according to the National Bureau of Economic Research.

However, many independently living seniors still need some type of caregiving assistance. SCAN surveyed 1,453 members, averaging age 82: None lived in a nursing home, despite meeting state qualifications. The survey found that 76% rely on a caregiver for assistance with daily activities. In 39.5% of these situations, the primary caregiver is a son or daughter.

The Facts of Long-Term Life

Consider the following concluding statistics:

- In the twenty-first century, one in five Americans will be 65 or older. One in nine current baby boomers will live to at least age 90. The number of those 85 years old and over will quadruple by 2050.

- About 6.5 million older people need assistance with activities of daily living (e.g., bathing, cooking, cleaning, dressing). That number is expected to double by 2020.

- Women account for 72% (18 million) of the approximately 25 million family caregivers in the United States.

- The U.S. Census Bureau projects that the number of caregivers will drop from 11 for each person needing long-term care in 1990 to four in 2050.

- Collectively, family caregivers spend $2 billion of their own assets each month to assist relatives.

- By 2005, non-institutionalized people over age 65 may spend an average of $14,000 annually on health care.

- Nearly 90% of baby boomers say taking care of their parents is among their top three life priorities.

- Ninety-four percent of seniors believe their health conditions do not affect their adult children's quality of life, but 80% of children say they do.

- Less than one-quarter of seniors expect to move in with their children; more than half of baby boomers anticipate having their parents move in at some point.

- Eighty-one percent of seniors do not believe their children will have to provide a great deal of financial support for their care; one-third of children believe they will.

The number of older Americans is increasing rapidly, while the human and financial resources to care for them are dwindling. Clearly then, elder care will become a major political issue in local, state, and national elections in the decades ahead.

Elder Care Resource Book: Options for Compassionate Care

A new guidebook offers a wealth of practical information on caregiving for seniors and their families. *Elder Care for the Millennium* by Bonnie L. Robeson and Lisa Mienville provides detailed information about legal matters and living options.

Simply making the home environment safe and comfortable for an older person needing care is one of the practical matters the book addresses. Some tips include making sure the lighting is bright – 100- to 200-watt bulbs are recommended; making sure there are handrails in bathrooms and hallways; installing low-pile carpet; using unbreakable dishes; and having a telephone by the bed.

The guide also includes directories of useful government agencies, associations, and companies providing specialized elder care supplies and equipment.

Source: *Elder Care for the Millennium: A Practical and Compassionate Guide for Caregiving* by Lisa Mienville and Bonnie L. Robeson. Graphix III Productions, 9521 Hickory Limb, Columbia, MD 21045. Telephone 1-410-381-5699; Web site www.edlercareplanning.com. 1999. 173 pages. Spiralbound. $19.95. (Order online from www.wfs.org/specials.htm.)

ABOUT THE AUTHOR Sam L. Ervin is the founder, chairman, president, and CEO of SCAN, an innovative health care plan for seniors. He has also served as a planning consultant for the United Way and as a consultant to the California Department on Aging. His address is SCAN Health Plan, P.O. Box 22616, Long Beach, CA 90801. Telephone 1-562-989-5118; Web site www.scanhealthplan.com.

Appendix D

Your Personal Papers Organizer

The following pages are meant to get you started with your life planning. You may choose do a complete plan for each family member, or combine all members into one document. Remember though, this is a living document and will change dramatically as family dynamics such as marriage, death, divorce occur.

Because this is a living document, you will be changing portions of it with each stage of life, i.e., marriage, births, deaths, divorce, relocation, etc. Get in the habit of reviewing this book on an annual basis and updating it as circumstances change. It is imperative that information be as current and as accurate as possible or it will be of no use to a family member in time of crisis.

The most important thing is that you get started. It doesn't have to be perfect – in fact, it never will be perfect. Because if it stops changing, you are no longer among the living.

To receive a CD of this organizer in 8.2 x 11 layout and in Word for Windows or pdf format, please use the order form on page 211.

Personal Records
and
Important Papers

For:

_____
(name)

This binder contains information on insurance, estate plan, wills and other items concerning my household.

Last date revised: _____

Important Phone Numbers and Contact Information

Primary Care Physician(s):

Who	Dr. Name	Address	Phone

Other Physicians/Specialists: (Optometrists, Chiropractors, etc.)

Who	Dr. Name	Address	Phone

Dentists:

Who	Dr. Name	Address	Phone

Other Contacts:

Who	Dr. Name	Address	Phone

Attorney _____

Financial Advisor _____

CPA/Tax Accountant _____

Other _____

Real Estate

(Include time share and other vacation property and unimproved land)

Description of Property: _____
Location:_____
Deed in Name of: _____
Location of Deed:_____
Deed Recorded:_____ Book: _____ Page:_____
Mortgage Face Amount: $_____ Type:_____
Payment:_____ Per: _____ Interest Rate:_____
Purchase Date:_____ Period of Payment:_____
Notes:_____

Description of Property: _____
Location: _____
Deed in Name of: _____
Location of Deed: _____
Deed Recorded:_____ Book:_____ Page:_____
Mortgage Face Amount: $_____ Type: _____
Payment:_____ Per:_____ Interest Rate:_____
Purchase Date:_____ Period of Payment:_____
Notes: _____

Description of Property: _____
Location: _____
Deed in Name of: _____
Location of Deed: _____
Deed Recorded:_____ Book: _____ Page:_____
Mortgage Face Amount: $_____ Type:_____
Payment: _____ Per: _____ Interest Rate: _____
Purchase Date:_____ Period of Payment: _____
Notes: _____

Credit Cards:
List all credit cards including department store, gasoline, etc.

Bank: _____ Type:* _____

Card #: _____ Credit Limit: _____

Customer Service Phone # _____

Note: Hide PIN # elsewhere and do not write expiration date here

---

Bank: _____ Type* _____

Card #: _____ Credit Limit: _____

Customer Service Phone # _____

Note: Hide PIN # elsewhere and do not write expiration date here.

Bank: _____ Type* _____

Card #: _____ Credit Limit: _____

Customer Service Phone # _____

Note: Hide PIN # elsewhere and do not write expiration date here.

Bank: _____ Type* _____

Card #: _____ Credit Limit: _____

Customer Service Phone # _____

Note: Hide PIN # elsewhere and do not write expiration date here.

Bank: _____ Type* _____

Card #: _____ Credit Limit: _____

Customer Service Phone # _____

Note: Hide PIN # elsewhere and do not write expiration date here.

* Type = Visa, MasterCard, AmEx, department store, etc.

Bank Accounts and Investments

Note: Use this section for information on bank accounts, Savings & Loan
   accounts, mutual fund shares, securities, investment clubs, savings bonds, etc.

Bank Account (Record PIN # elsewhere)

Name of Bank: _____ Type of Account: _____

Address _____

Phone _____ Contact Name: _____

Account #: _____ Bank Card # _____

Web address for on-line banking: _____

NOTES: _____

_____

Bank Account (Record PIN # elsewhere)

Name of Bank: _____ Type of Account: _____

Address _____

Phone _____ Contact Name: _____

Account #: _____ Bank Card # _____

Web address for on-line banking: _____

NOTES: _____

_____

Bank Account (Record PIN # elsewhere)

Name of Bank: _____ Type of Account: _____

Address _____

Phone _____ Contact Name: _____

Account #: _____ Bank Card # _____

Web address for on-line banking: _____

NOTES: _____

_____

Investments

Name of Investment: _____ Type of Investment*: _____

Address: _____

Phone: _____ Contact Name: _____

Account #: _____ Term of Contract: _____

Location of certificate/contract/etc.: _____

NOTES: _____

_____

Investments

Name of Investment: _____ Type of Investment*: _____

Address: _____

Phone: _____ Contact Name: _____

Account #: _____ Term of Contract: _____

Location of certificate/contract/etc.: _____

NOTES: _____

_____

Investments

Name of Investment: _____ Type of Investment*: _____

Address: _____

Phone: _____ Contact Name: _____

Account #: _____ Term of Contract: _____

Location of certificate/contract/etc.: _____

NOTES: _____

_____

* Mutual Fund, Stocks, Bonds, Annuities

Insurance Quick Reference Directory

(Details of policies listed below can be found on successive pages herein)

Company	Type of Insurance*	Policy #	Agent	Phone #

* = Property, Auto, personal property, life, supplemental health, long-term care

Life Insurance

Name of Insured:_____ Type of Policy:[1]_____

Carrier: _____ Policy #: _____

Date of Policy: _____ Face Amount: $ _____

Premium $: _____Per:[2]____ Policy located: _____

Beneficiary(ies): _____

Agent: _____ Phone:_____

Address:_____

Notes: _____

_____

Long Term Care Insurance

Name of Insured: _____ Type of Policy:[1]_____

Carrier: _____ Policy #: _____

Date of Policy: _____ Coverage: $ _____

Premium $: _____Per:[2]____ Policy located: _____

Beneficiary(ies): _____

Agent:_____ Phone: _____

Address: _____

Notes: _____

_____

[1] Term, Whole, Universal
[2] Month, Quarter, Year

Property Insurance
Home, vacation home, household items, boats, jewelry, etc.

Property Covered: _____

Carrier: _____ Policy #:_____

Address: _____ Phone:_____

Agent:_____ Phone: _____

Premium paid with house pmt.? Yes__ No___ Amount $:_____

Notes: _____

Property Covered: _____

Carrier: _____ Policy #: _____

Address: _____ Phone: _____

Agent:_____ Phone: _____

Premium paid with house pmt.? Yes__ No___ Amount $:_____

Notes: _____

Vehicle Insurance: (Cars, Trucks, RVs)

Carrier:_____ Phone: _____

Address:_____

Agent: _____ Notes:_____

#1 Vehicle ID #_____ License Plate #_____

#2 Vehicle ID #_____ License Plate #_____

#3 Vehicle ID #_____ License Plate #_____

#4 Vehicle ID #_____ License Plate #_____

#5 Vehicle ID #_____ License Plate #_____

Driver's License Information

Name: _____ License # _____

Name: _____ License #_____

Name: _____ License #_____

Health Insurance

Insurance Company:_____ Phone #:_____

Employer: _____ Group #:_____

Person Insured:_____ Policy #:_____

Name	ID #	Coverage Notes

Dental Insurance

Insurance Company:_____ Phone #:_____

Address: _____ Policy #: _____

Notes: _____

Vision Insurance

Insurance Company:_____ Phone #:_____

Address: _____ Policy #: _____

Notes: _____

Supplemental Insurance   (Long Term Care, Cancer, Disability, etc.)

Name of Insured:_____

Insurance Company: _____ Phone #: _____

Address: _____ Policy #:_____

Notes: _____

Name of Insured:_____

Insurance Company: _____ Phone #: _____

Address: _____ Policy #:_____

Notes: _____

Household Inventory

In case of fire, tornado, or other loss, you and the claims' representative will need to know the value of your household goods and personal property to settle your claim. Go room by room through your home and garage and list all items of furniture, appliances, paintings, record albums, CDs, DVDs, videos, etc. Take pictures of antiques, expensive jewelry or artifacts of value. Keep these pictures with your records. If receipts are available, store them in this section.

Item	Model #	Serial #	Original Cost	Year Purchased

Location Directory (List the location of all important documents)

Bank Records:	
Certificates of Deposit:	
Stock and Bond Certificates:	
Savings Bonds:	
Tax Records:	
Bills of Sale:	
Promissory Notes:	
Property Deeds & Mortgage Papers:	
Safety Deposit Box and Key:	
Wills and/or Trusts:	
Copies of Wills and/or Trusts:	
Powers of Attorney:	
Health Care Directives:	
Insurance Policies:	
Vehicle Titles and Registrations:	
Social Security Cards:	
Passports:	
Birth Certificates:	
Marriage Certificates:	
Adoption Papers:	
Divorce Decrees:	
Military Papers:	
Diplomas:	
Family Pictures:	
Genealogy:	
Warranties and Guarantees:	
Other:	

Military Service Information and Organization/Association

Memberships

Military:

Name of Family Member:_____

Years of Service: _____ Rank: _____

Honors: _____

Benefits Entitled To: _____

_____

Organizations/Associations:

Name of Family Member: _____

Name of Organization: _____

Contact Name: _____ Phone #: _____

Address: _____

Notes: _____

_____

Name of Family Member: _____

Name of Organization: _____

Contact Name: _____ Phone #: _____

Address: _____

Notes: _____

_____

Medical History: (Use one sheet for each family member)

Name: _____ Birth Date: _____

Birth Place: _____ Blood Type: _____

Insurance Medical Record #: _____

Doctors Names:	Phone & addresses

Allergies, broken bones, surgery:

Shots and Immunizations: Type	Date:

Illnesses: Type:	Date:

Notes:

About the Author

Linda Thompson, founder and president of *Planning for Tomorrow* has over 30 years marketing experience working for companies such as Motorola and Honeywell. Linda left the corporate world in 1998 to pursue self-employment. She obtained her securities and insurance licenses and began selling life insurance and investment products.

While working with her clients, she realized the need to assist those who were facing the challenges of working caregivers. Calling on her contacts in the elder care industry, she formed a team of professionals who could assist those clients in all aspects of *life planning* from elder care to retirement planning; from end-of-life planning to family communication and counseling. From that foundation *Planning for Tomorrow* was created.

Determining that her passion lie not in the financial services world but in the education arena, she developed a series of workshops and lectures focused on *life planning*, specifically targeting the Baby Boomer generation. For over four years, she has offered these lectures and workshops to companies for their employees. This series of brown-bag-lunch sessions has been well received, and in some cases, was standing room only.

During this same time, she and her mother made the decision to build and share a home in the Phoenix, AZ area. That decision began Linda's entrée into the world of the working caregiver. With the advent of *Planning for Tomorrow*, she and her mother agreed to share their personal journey as described within.

The next logical move for Linda was a book and *Planning for Tomorrow – Your Passport to a Confident Future*, is the compilation of these lectures, research, and Linda's personal life experiences. It is Linda's hope that readers of this book will determine a need to develop their own *life plan* and that it will help them create that plan.

Linda can be reached at:
Life Path Solutions
PMB404, #106
2487 S. Gilbert Road
Gilbert, AZ 85296-5802
Phone: (480) 899-8647
e-mail: Linda.Thompson@pft-az.com
Web site: www.pft-az.com

Resources

Over the years, I've come across some absolutely wonderful booklets, designed to help an individual or family with their *life plan*. Some of these booklets are focused on family meetings and how to conduct them; some are actual documents that can become a part of your life plan; and some are merely informational on a specific subject. Some are free and some are not. Below is a list of those that may be most helpful to you. This list is in no way meant to be comprehensive nor does it list every organization and/or booklet available.

Booklet Sources

AARP
602 F. Street, NW, Washington DC 20049
www.aarp.org
"Family Conversations that Help Parents Stay Independent"

Health Care Decisions
1510 E. Flower, Phoenix, AZ 85014
www.hcdecisions.org
"Facts About Health Care Decisions"

National Association of Insurance Commissioners
2301 McGee Street, #800, Kansas City, MO 64108-2604
www.naic.org
"A Shopper's Guide to Long-Term Care Insurance"

Aging with Dignity
PO Box 1661, Tallahassee, FL 32302-1661
www.agingwithdignity.org
"Five Wishes"

National Cremation Society,
A subsidiary of SCI Management,
1929 Allen Parkway, Houston, TX 77019
www.nationalcremation.com
"That's My Wish, A Personal Planning Guide"

Additional Reading Recommendations

1. Conrad, Richard T. What Should we do About Mom: A New Look at Growing Old. Human Services Institute, TAB Books, 1993

2. Mills, Daniel Quinn. Not Like Our Parents: How the Baby Boom Generation is Changing America. William Morrow and Company, 1987

3. The MetLife Survey of American Attitudes Towards Retirement. Conducted by Zogby International, 2001, for MetLife Mature Market Institute

4. Puchta, Charles. The Aging America Resources Guide. Aging America Resources, 2002

5. Freedman, Marc. Prime Time, How baby boomers will Revolutionize Retirement and Transform America. Public Affairs Books, 1999

6. Dychtwald, Ken and Flower, Joe. Age Wage, How the Most Important Trend of Our Time Will Change Your Future. Bantam Books, 1990

7. Dychtwald, Ken. Age Power, How the 21st Century will be Ruled by the New Old. Penguin Putnam Inc. 1999

8. Smith, J. Walker and Clurman, Ann. Rocking the Ages. Harper Collins. 1998

9. Gillon, Steve. Boomer Nation:The Largest and Richest Generation Ever, and How It Changed America. Free Press. 2004

Order Form

To order additional copies of *Planning for Tomorrow – Your Passport to a Confident Future*, complete the information below:

Ship to: (please print)

Name: _____

Address: _____

City/State/Zip:_____

Day Phone: _____

Planning for Tomorrow – Your Passport to a Confident Future:

_____ copies of book @ $39.95 ea. $_____

Shipping & Handling @ $5.00 per book $_____

Arizona residents add 5.6% tax ($2.24/ book) $_____

Total Amount enclosed $ _____

Make checks payable to: **Linda Thompson**

Mail to:

Life Path Solutions
PMB404, #106
2487 S. Gilbert Rd.
Gilbert, AZ 85296-5802

A *Planning for Tomorrow* Personal Papers Organizer CD will be enclosed with each book shipped.

Bulk orders may be ordered at a discounted rate. Please call us at 480-899-8647 for details.

Organizer CD Order Form

If you purchased this book in a retail establishment, you did not receive the Personal Papers Organizer CD. To order your free CD of the *Planning for Tomorrow* Personal Papers Organizer, please complete the information below:

Ship to: (please print)

Name: _____

Address: _____

City/State/Zip:_____

Day Phone: _____

Fax to: *Planning for Tomorrow* Organizer
                 (480) 917-0702

or

Mail to: Life Path Solutions
                 PMB404, #106
                 2487 S. Gilbert Rd.
                 Gilbert, AZ 85296-5802

or

Contact us throughour website at: www.pft-az.com

Only one CD per order, please.

Printed in the United States
26161LVS00005B/181-360